NO WAY OUT

Roberto Valenza

No Way Out

(Conversations with U.G. Krishnamurti)

Foreword by
MAHESH BHATT

Editors
J.S.L.R. NARAYANA MOORTY
ANTONY PAUL FRANK NORONHA
SUNITA PANT BANSAL

Smriti Books
New Delhi (INDIA)

My teaching, if that is the word you want to use, has no copyright. You are free to reproduce, distribute, interpret, misinterpret, distort, garble, do what you like, even claim authorship, without my consent or the permission of anybody.

U. G.

ISBN: 81-87967-08-0

First Edition: 2002

© Design and Presentation: Smriti Books

Cover Design: Shaiju Mathew

Pictures: Courtesy Julie Thayer

Publishers

SMRITI BOOKS

Email: smritibooks@vsnl.net

Website: www.spbenterprises.com

Distributors

NEW AGE BOOKS

A-44 Naraina Phase I

New Delhi-110 028 (INDIA)

Email: nab@vsnl.in

Website: www.newagebooksindia.com

Printed in India

by Jainendra Prakash Jain at Shri Jainendra Press

A-45 Naraina Phase-I New Delhi-110 028 (INDIA)

Publisher's Note

I asked a friend, an editor of a magazine, to do a cover story on U.G. His prompt response was, "U.G. is not a cover story material, he is only for the upper-class intellectuals...has no mass appeal..." "Very few people can understand him and his philosophy," he went on to add.

On coming out of his office, I pondered over the startling revelation. After all, just because I understood or appreciated something, does not mean that everyone else does too.

I started going through the various material available on / about U.G. and discovered that the fault did not lie with U.G. or his statements (which I knew already) but with people like us who want to present him to the world.

Just like when we present a rose to someone, we break off all its thorns, we should present the essence of U.G.'s philosophy in its purity, minus the mind-shattering, devastating, blasphemous...thorns.

I am trying to do this exercise and hope to reach the masses!

Sunita Pant Bansal
NOIDA, India
2002

Contents

Foreword

"At least 2,000 Muslims have died in the violence which erupted all over Gujarat after the Godhra massacre," said my young Muslim driver. I was driving through the riot battered streets of Ahmedabad. The sight of burnt mosques and smashed shops looked bizarre in the glow of the pre-dawn light. The clock on the dashboard of his cab, that sat next to the holy picture of Mecca, showed 6.20 a.m.

"My father, who was trying to save us, was caught by the mob and asked to say 'Jai Sri Ram'; when he refused, they cut him up and burnt him right in front of me," he said looking me straight in the eye. I was jolted by his starkness.

As the day deepened I visited an overcrowded relief camp where I met hundreds of riot victims who told me tales of unspeakable violence that was unleashed against them by the goons of the Vishwa Hindu Parishad and the Bajrang Dal. But what staggered me the most was that these heinous acts were perpetrated with the sanction of the State and the local police. Never in my life I had felt or touched human anguish of this magnitude. So I did what I always do when I come to the end of my tether. I called UG.

" UG, India is falling apart! Is there anything one can do to prevent it from going to pieces? Is there a glue that can keep us together?" I asked with wholehearted desperation.

"What happens if the whole thing falls apart? Why are you frightened of the chaos that may result? Why do you want to hold on to things exactly the way they are? Your Gurus have been marketing all kinds of glues to you for centuries to keep your world intact. Have they helped? Mahesh, if this great heritage which you all are so proud of has produced monsters like these, who are killing people in the name of God, don't you think its time you should dump that great heritage into the garbage bin? Can you still go on shamelessly bragging to the world that India is the Mother of all civilizations? " He asked with child like purity, before hanging up. His words brought tears to my eyes. I was reminded of an intense conversation I had with him during the winter of 1989 in Bangalore.

The conversation

Myself: What is your message to the mankind?

U.G.: I have no message for mankind —I cannot help you. You are doomed. Go back to whatever you are doing. Your religion, your guru, your drugs, your comforts. Live in misery and die in misery. Whatever I am saying has no religious content. I don't want to be stigmatized as a religious teacher. You first stick that filthy label of enlightenment on me and then judge my actions according to that. How can you call me a Godman when I say God is irrelevant? Go to your Gurus and buy comfort from them. I don't give a damn for all those teachers who existed before me. I am going to say that until the end of my days. They were con men, they conned themselves and conned the whole of mankind and we are going to pay a heavy price for their con game.

Myself: Do you mean to say all the leaders of mankind falsified themselves?

UG: Has their teaching produced any results? The teachers of mankind created the misery. If humanity has to be saved from the chaos of its own making, it has to be saved from the saviours of mankind, and I am not one of them. Why should nature or some cosmic power, if there is one in the world, need the help of somebody as an instrument to help others? You are as much an expression of that power. Every dog, every pig, everybody, you, me and even Hitler was an expression of the same thing.

Myself: Don't you see that you are destroying the very foundation of human thought? You are taking away from us our sense of purpose.

U G: Life is fire. It does not tolerate anything dead. Your ideas are dead. They falsify life. Every thought is fascist in its nature—anything born out of thought is destructive. The whole foundation of our civilization is built on the foundation to kill and to be killed – in the name of God symbolized by the church and all the other religious institutions and in the name of political ideologies symbolized by the State. Man is expendable.

Myself: Where do you think we are going UG?

UG: We are moving progressively in the direction of total destruction.

Myself: In short we are doomed?

UG: The obvious need not be restated. No *Avtar*, no Guru, no Godman can stop this from happening.

As you read this book many of you will feel that you are being robbed of all those fragile certainties, which you took a lifetime to gather. Let me forewarn you. U G 's words are like fire; they will burn you. But strangely they will also leave you rejuvenated.

Mahesh Bhatt
Mumbai, India
2002

Preface

Trying to understand U.G. or his teachings is like trying to grasp the wind in the palm of your hand. Though they are as refreshing and fragrant as a fresh breeze, yet they can also be as devastating as a wild fire! They are as nourishing as the earth and water, if only we can just listen to them and then 'forget all about them'! U.G.'s teachings can certainly bring us down to earth from the lofty but cloudy skies of illusion, so that we can come back and live a 'simple and ordinary life' of peace without struggle or conflict!

I am writing the following in the spirit of revealing a progression in the consciousness of someone who is exposed to U.G. and/or his teachings and who tries to integrate them into his own living. My conclusion will also perhaps reveal the limitation of the conscious mind when trying to resolve the questions and paradoxes it finds. In writing this, I feel that I am probably speaking for a number of others who are in the same boat as I am.

It is difficult to assess U.G.'s teachings without discussing his persona and his lifestyle, for the possibilities he presents would remain vague without a living example to refer to. In fact, U.G. himself connects his teachings with what has happened to him and how he lives. It's also difficult to talk about U.G.'s teachings or study them without being affected by them, without relating them to oneself. Add to this the fact that people who have been acquainted with U.G. personally cannot but relate his teaching to what they observe of him, to their relationship with him, and to how that has affected them.

Even then the teachings leave the reader wondering about some questions. Maybe there is never a resolution of these questions. Maybe life, as U.G. might say, can never be understood. And may be, again as U.G. would put it, all attempts to understand life are only expressions of the one and only theme of human thinking: to protect and maintain the self.

One thing I can say personally after being acquainted with U.G. and his teachings for more than a decade is this: I am in no position to accept or reject his teachings. They can neither be proven nor disproven; and in what follows I shall try to explain why it does not matter that one cannot do so. Let me first present in a few paragraphs what a reader might glean as to the basics of the philosophy in U.G.'s teachings.

U.G. presents the problems generated by what he calls the 'stranglehold of thought' (or of culture) on the human being; that is, by creating the self and separating the individual from the world around him or her, thought or culture is responsible for a duplicate life of the individual, a life not intimately connected with, but in fact far removed from the actual world of the body or the living organism and its environment. This duplicate life in turn results in man's self-centeredness and destructiveness.

While the only interest of the living organism is to survive (for the moment) and reproduce itself (or as U.G. would say, to produce one like itself), the interest of the thought world is to maintain itself. Thought maintains itself by translating each experience in terms of past experiences, interpreting it as pleasant or painful, and pursuing it if it finds it pleasant and avoiding it if it finds it painful. Each experience creates a fictitious idea of the self in us by seeking continuity of it-self, by demanding to be repeated through what U.G. calls "the pleasure movement". For instance, when a past experience presents itself in the present moment as desirable, it also simultaneously creates the idea of the self for which the experience is desirable.

The self, however, is not a real entity, nor is there any entity called the mind, which is really another name for the self, nor is there something called pure consciousness, for there is no consciousness which does not involve a translation or interpretation of what it is conscious of, and hence which does not involve a self.

In fact the experience which is seen as pleasant and which tries to perpetuate itself is the self. The division between the self and the experience is one of the mischievous creations of thought. Thought 'builds' on experience and creates the desire for 'ultimate happiness', or, as U.G. would say, "a desire for permanent happiness without a moment of pain". The resulting duplicate life creates self-centeredness and self-protectiveness.

U.G. says that the self-centeredness created by thought will do everything to maintain itself, even at the expense of the destruction of the world, and the destruction of the very living organism on which thought is based, as witnessed by people who wage wars, and who kill others or themselves for the sake of an idea.

All this seems to be logical until we come to what U.G. has to say about how we can get out of this situation: U.G. says there is no way out! All attempts at our part to become free from the stranglehold of thought only perpetuate the self, entrench us more deeply in it. All attempts at improving the self, at detachment or renunciation, positive or negative thinking, understanding, knowledge, meditation, religious or spiritual pursuits, social reform or revolution – all of these, being initiated by thought, can only maintain and strengthen the self. Thus, they do not free us. "The only freedom there is, is to be free from the very idea of freedom."

U.G., however, does say that when somehow this realization sinks into us, when the whole field (of the self?) is exhausted, then a physiological mutation can take place. When this occurs the living organism is freed from the stranglehold of thought and returns to its naturally peaceful condition. Thought then "falls into its natural rhythm" by coming into active function only when it is needed in a situation. But this is not something that can be caused by any 'effort or volition' on your or my part. In fact the necessary condition for it to happen is for all effort to cease.

How do we understand this sort of teaching? If there is nothing one can do after listening to U.G., if the whole problem of our existence arose out of our desire structure, can we at least give up the whole enterprise of seeking fulfillment and "go home"? Of course, we realize the paradox to trying to abandon seeking is itself based on the motive of becoming free from our problems, which is in the first place a self-centered concern. But we see no choice; and we try to let go of the concern and return to our normal routine life. We, in the process, even try to "drop" U.G. from our consciousness; for U.G. is only a symbol for all that we have been seeking to fulfill ourselves. And when U.G. is gone, the rest is gone too. All the things we seek for our fulfillment, including U.G., are nothing but ourselves. That is why, when they (and U.G.) are gone, the self is gone too.

Let me recall, in this context, a conversation I recently had with U.G., "I have always been open to you; I feel that as far as I am concerned, if anything has to go (meaning taken away from me, as a result of my knowing U.G.), including myself, in the process, that's fine with me. It does not matter. That's why I have no resistance to you." Then U.G. said in reply, "If you go, then I go, Sir!" Meaning that when I can let myself go, then U.G. would lose all significance in my consciousness.

But before we ever try this approach, we normally go through many questions, and raise criticisms and objections to U.G.'s teachings in our attempts to integrate U.G.'s teachings into our lives. I will maintain a few of the questions that occurred to me.

1) When U.G. says that for him thought comes into action only when a given situation demands it, where is the demarcating line between what the situation itself demands, and what I (assuming that I am U.G. for the moment) demand of the situation? When someone, for instance, asks me a question, or makes a request, I say something to him in response (my response, as U.G. would say, coming from my conditioning). Suppose he is not satisfied with my response, but later comes back with the same question or demand. Now, do I have a situation to respond to, or is it my own need (coming perhaps from my conditioning, say, of proving myself, or not parting with my money easily), which somehow presses me to further reply to him? Is my second response just a response elicited by the situation or is it my previous response demanding to repeat itself? How can I tell the difference?

Or, to put the same difficulty in other words, it is not clear how one could make sense of U.G.'s idea that there is no "build-up" (of responses to situations) with him. U.G. himself says that there is a wish or desire in him only where he sees the means to satisfy it. But the question is, how can he (or I in his place) know that there are means unless I have a desire to satisfy in the first place? How is such a situation different from my desiring things, and being flexible enough to change the desire or let go of it when things don't go my way?

2) Again, U.G. calls his state a state of unknowing. How can he himself make any statements about it without knowing something about it? U.G. would say that he does not know it, but rather that he is only speaking conventionally or metaphorically, or that he is merely *denying* that his is a state of knowing; that is why he makes such statements, not that he actually knows anything about it. Or, he says that with him both knowing and not knowing occur 'in the same frame'. Or sometimes he says that it is life expressing itself (through this sort of language?), and he does not know. And he has no desire to know or make any sense out of anything. He would in fact claim that it is our urge to know, and make sense of things, that is the problem, because it is that that is building the self. He is certain, as far as he is concerned, that there is nothing to know, nothing to understand. Except he can't communicate that certainty to us. But how does he know that he does not know? How does he know that his is (or was) *not* a state of knowing?

3) In our normal daily life many activities we undertake are initiated in our consciousness by the thought of what we ought to do or are going to do. When U.G. says that the situation brings about the thought, does that mean that he is just a victim of the situation, and that so as far as he is concerned anything can happen? Or, in him too, is there a consciousness of the situation,

and a deliberation as to what is appropriate to it? If the latter is the case, then how is he different from us?

Of course, it is also true that we often spontaneously respond to situations without prior deliberation or forethought, even if the response happens to be just saying something. We don't always think first and then act. Is U.G. the same always, i.e. spontaneous?

4) Or again, when a thought occurs, there is also an accompanying consciousness of ourselves within us, even if it is only momentary and not connected to a previous consciousness (or experiences) through memory. If a thought occurs in U.G.'s consciousness in a certain situation, how can it not bring out a consciousness of himself, and hence an image of himself, however momentary it may be? U.G. might say that "there is knowing and there is not knowing in the same frame"; but how are we to understand that? If there is that self-consciousness in him, then it seems that the difference between U.G. and us is only a matter of degree, that degree (which seems to be great) being determined by how much we are able to let go of the past, or accept the present. Then, couldn't we just practice letting go or acceptance either through meditation or some other processes and thereby approximate to U.G.'s condition? If it is possible, this seems to be in direct contradiction to what U.G. says about how there is nothing we can do – either this condition just happens, or it doesn't. But again, we don't know the facts of the matter, because we are not there.

5) Further, we have no way of making sense of U.G.'s assertions that "it never occurs to me that you are separate or different from me," for in this speech and in his day-to-day dealings he has to be making those distinctions.

Now I am aware, after I raise the above sort of difficulties with U.G.'s teachings that the problems may not be with U.G. or his teachings. The problem may be that I am trying to understand what is to me unknown from my own point of view, and perhaps there is no way I can do that unless and until I give it up! All these difficulties may simply disappear in the face of the reality of U.G., and his actual living, if it happens to be otherwise. Somehow it may all 'fit'. We just don't know how. Thus we can neither prove nor disprove (nor can U.G.) U.G.'s teachings. We are not in any position to confirm or deny what he says. Even the language he speaks leaves us baffled. There is nothing in our background or mental equipment to relate to it. Sometime you even wonder if you are speaking the same language. Even the very possibility of any communication is in question.

A new dialectic builds up in this context: the reader asks for coherence in and explanation of U.G.'s statements, and U.G. retorts that the urge to know, to seek explanations or coherence (from him) is how thought is building the self. This is how, he would say, the intellect is the strengthening itself. And he would add that the intellect is the only instrument of understanding, and there is no other instrument. Furthermore, another part of U.G.'s 'certainty' is that there is really nothing to understand! To the seeker the concern about the self seems irrelevant; but U.G. maintains that it is the seeker's main interest. He says there are no disinterested pursuits. In this controversy, I personally agree with U.G.'s position. How can I not do so, if I understand and see the analysis he presents of human problems?

Turning to the subject of U.G.'s persona and his lifestyle, things are just as ambiguous: it is not clear to what extent his living reflects his teachings. Again, here too, the urge to verify, to make sense out of his life, is, as U.G. would point out, expressive of our concern for the self. U.G.'s living, just as his statement, does not fit any fixed pattern. On the one hand, he seems to be living in a discontinuous state of consciousness, where what happens one moment is disconnected, or 'disjointed' as U.G. himself would put it, from the next; on the other hand, he can not only remember an infinite number of details of his own past (and endlessly talk about them), but also is able to plan his trips or meetings with people, which all seems to indicate a process of stringing various events sequentially in a single consciousness. This is, as far as we know, indicative of the process of self-making.

This same paradox is also evident in at least some of the dialogue included in this book. On the one hand, the conversations proceed in a free-association style, as U.G. goes from one topic to another and answers questions without any rule or rhyme, sometimes without directly answering the questions posed to him. However this may appear, the main themes of U.G.'s teachings seem to come out of the conversations anyway, although it would appear to the listener that U.G. is more interested in trying to 'grind his axe' rather than answering the questions. On the other hand, U.G. is quite capable of a sustained conversation on a single topic, as can be evidenced in his interview with a scientist. He can go in depth and focus on a problem and bring it to a conclusion, usually by cornering his listener in some fashion or other (by making remarks such as, in the above example, "What will you do, Sir?").

U.G.'s personal life is quite casual and informal. There is usually a party-like atmosphere around him. Wherever one sees him, he is generally surrounded by one or more of his friends, whom he constantly jokes with and teases and who in turn do the same to him. When a stranger walks in, U.G. instantly cuts out all the jocularity, becomes serious and sits quietly, and waits for the visitor to start talking, after a few courtesies. Pretty soon, the visitor is dragged into the network of U.G.'s thought. It is very hard to escape the effects of U.G.'s conversations. You may end up joking around with him, or you may get upset with the result that both you and U.G. yell back and forth at each other, or you can't stand it anymore and leave the scene! There is no set pattern as to how a visitor would react to U.G. Of course, there are also those who think that U.G. and his teachings are phony.

But you do know that when you talk to U.G. your very existence is in question. That is probably the reason why some people feel quite threatened in U.G.'s presence. U.G. not only exposes all sorts of hidden motivations in what you have said, but he also negates most of what people say, trying to dislodge their belief structure, using whatever means he has at his disposal. He knows that all beliefs are relative, and uses the relativity of belief to combat belief. In other words, he uses one belief to counter another belief, and then in another context he uses the second belief to counter the first. He does not hold to rules of consistency. Nothing is so sacrosanct for him that it has to be protected at all costs!

U.G.'s personal relationships (if that's what one can call them) are no exceptions to the above rule (or rather the absence of it). Sometimes he would seem to personally want to see you and would seem to care for you. (How many times one hasn't heard the remark from different people that no one cared for them as much as U.G. did?) He may call you or come to see you; he chats or jokes with you, eats with you, and so on. Yet, it looks like after he leaves, he rarely thinks about you again, (except when people talk about you, or in conversation, he would remember you). On the one side, he seems not to care how you live, whom you see, and so on, yet, on other side, you will find him meddling with people's lives, teasing them and attacking them.

How does U.G. the person tally with U.G.'s teachings; does he live up to them? Of course, it's not a problem for U.G. You never hear him complaining about his life. (That's for sure). He says that the thought never occurs to him that he should be in a different state than the state he is in. When he is sick, he does not complain. Again, on the other hand, there are exceptions to this. Although he does not normally go to a doctor on his own, he does consult doctors, (maybe only because there is a doctor on hand) to find out what they have to say about his condition. Not that he carries out their advice. U.G. says he does not live up to anyone's image of him (including the image of an *enlightened* man).

Many times he gives you the impression he is the most disinterested man in the world. He does not wish to change or convert anyone. Then why is he so concerned about some teachers like J. Krishnamurti? Why does he involve himself in controversies, or put down "everyone and everything"? Of course, he would say that he is only responding to you, coming to him and asking him all these questions. He by himself has no desire to say anything. You cannot but think of attributing various motives to him, such as seeking popularity, trying to succeed in competition, and so forth. At the same time, when you look at a picture of him looking at you, those eyes full of love, all your doubts and questions disappear. How does one deal with a person like U.G.?

All this ultimately boils down to an ambivalence which in fact hides a fundamental contradiction in the reader (the present writer including): You can't take U.G. for you don't know how to take him; for, as U.G. would put it, if you really understand what he says you would instantly drop dead, that would mean 'clinical death' (to your self, at any rate); and that you cannot afford. And you can't leave him alone, because all your thinking will eventually bring him into the picture, because he and his teaching represents the limits or end of seeking.

Since we cannot truly 'understand' and accept what he says, we end up with the following contradiction instead. Inasmuch as U.G. represents the end of seeking, we would like to make him and his teaching the object of our interest. But the only way we can relate to him and his teaching is in a self-centered fashion, trying to posses him (wish you luck in that!), patronizing him, bragging about him and his teaching, trying to get his approval and confirmation of what we say or write or do, and so on. If that does not work, we go to the opposite extreme of trying to be independent of him, criticizing him, attacking him, and so forth. Both sides of this ambivalence are movements of our own thought. Both represent ways of grasping something, or seeking. We are trying to get somewhere, to change ourselves into something we are not. When we are free from the seeking, then U.G. and his teachings do not matter. Then we can drop them. Perhaps later in another context we will talk to him or to someone else about him or his teachings, and then we will think about him and his teachings again. Then we may fall headlong into a pattern of ambivalence again, not realizing until later that we have. Then we may drop him again. If that "falling and rising" of our concern with U.G. doesn't matter, then it does not matter if we ourselves are related to U.G. or not, and then *it does not matter whether U.G.'s teachings are true or not.* You merely return to your normal daily routine, whatever it consists of. The routine may include the movement back and forth, say, of being concerned and not so concerned with U.G. and his teachings, just as, when we are not conscious of ourselves, there may be a movement back and forth between being involved in things and being bored. When we become conscious of ourselves, we may let everything (even our concern for our fulfillment or freedom) go, or accept our condition, or merely return to the present moment, which is one and the same thing. This indeed is our "condition" and as far as we know there may be no escape from it. But then if we are conscious of all this, we realize that this too is born of the need to become free and when we let that need go, we return to our normal routine, at least for the moment. Then as U.G. would say, "You can just as well take a walk." And there is nothing more to say….

J.S.R.L. Narayana Moorty
California, U.S.A.

The next few chapters are the various question-answer sessions with U.G. held in different parts of the world by many people.

Nothing To Be Transformed

Q : Is there any such thing as your own experience?

U.G.: Whatever you experience has already been experienced by someone else. Your telling yourself, "Ah! I am in a blissful state ", means that some one else before you has experienced that and had passed it on to you. Whatever may be the nature of the medium through which you experience, it is a second-hand, third-hand, and last-hand experience. It is not yours. There is no such thing as your own experience. Such experiences, however extraordinary, aren't worth a thing.

Q : But we get caught up with that idea.

U.G.: The experience is you.

Q : We want to know what truth is. We want to know that enlightment is.

U.G.: You already know it. Don't tell me that you don't. There is no such thing as truth at all.

Q : I don't know.

U.G.: You can only say that there is a logically ascertained premise called truth and you can write a book, "My Quest for Truth", like your ex-president Radhakrishnan.

Q : But you had this search. Was it real? You also didn't know what it was about.

U.G.: My case was quite different.

Q : How is that?

U.G.: I was thrown into that environment. I was surrounded by all the religious people. I had spent all my formative years in the milieu of the Theosophical Society. I didn't have anything to do with my own blood relatives. The only people that I knew were the leaders of the Theosophical Society. The old man Mr. J. Krishnamurti was part of my background. I did not go t him. In every room of our house we had photos of J.Krishnamurti, beginning from his ninth or tenth year till he was, I don't know how old. I disliked the photos of all gods and goddesses.

Q : You mean that was the background, which made you what you are today?

U.G.: No, no. I am saying that despite all that, whatever happened to me has happened. It seems a miracle. That is the reason why I emphasize without a shadow of doubt, that whatever has happened to me can happen to a con man, to a rapist, to a murderer, or to a thief. All of them have as much a chance as, if not a better one than, all these spiritual people put together. Don't ask me the question, "Was the Buddha a rapist, or Jesus something else?" That's not an intelligent question.

Q : Coming back to your earlier statement – what is it that you did in pursuance of your goal?

U.G.: You give me a list of all the saints, sages, and saviours of mankind. Then, look at their lives and look at what they did. I did everything they did. Nothing happened. I knew what it was all about. I was interested in finding out whether there was anything to all those teachers, from the very beginning of our times. I found out that they conned themselves and conned every one of us. Was there anything to their experience, which they wanted to share with the world?

Q : What do you think?

U.G.: Nothing. Don't ask me, "Why did they last for so long?" The Ivory soap or Pears soap in the United Stated is celebrating its 100th year. The fact that it lasted for a hundred years does not mean that there is anything to it. This certainty that they were all false, and their teachings falsified me, is something, which I cannot transmit to anyone. It is your problem. As I said this morning, I had this hunger, I had this thirst. Nothing satisfied my hunger and nothing satisfied my quest. You know, the old man [J. Krishnamurti] and I thrashed out everything for thirty days, whenever he could find time. We used to go for walks. I met him towards the end of my association with the Theosophical Society

Q : For some years he was close to you.

U.G.: No, no. I wanted to find out whether there was anything to him. He was saying something on the platform. Towards the end I asked him a question, "What do you have behind all the abstractions you are throwing at me and others? Is there anything?" (That was my way of dealing with problems.) I listened to him every time he came to Madras. But I didn't swallow any of his words. Then the encounter came about in a very strange way. We thrashed it out. I told him, "Look here, as far as thought is concerned, it has reached its acme in India. You can't even hold a candle before those mighty thinkers that India has produced. What it is that you have? I want an answer". But then we didn't get along. I said to myself, "You are nowhere. What the hell are you doing here?" I didn't want to waste my time. So I told the old man, "You can give your time to anyone who you think will be helped by you". And that finished the whole thing. That was in 1953. I never saw him afterwards.

Q : Sir, does all this [U.G.'s search and his 'calamity'] mean that there was a certain programming?

U.G.: If there is one, you have to rule out all such things as mutation, and radical transformation. I ruled those out because I didn't find anything there to be transformed. There was no question of mutation of mind, radical or otherwise. It is all hogwash. But it is difficult for you to throw all this stuff out of your system. You can also deny it and brush it aside, but this, "May be there is something to it," lasts for a long time. When once you stumble into a situation that you can call 'courage' you can throw the entire past out of yourself. I don't know how this has happened. What has happened is something which cannot but be called an act of courage, because everything, not only this or that particular teacher you had been involved with, but everything that every man, every person, thought, felt, and experienced before you, is completely flushed out of your system. What you are left with is the simple thing – the body with its extraordinary intelligence of its own.

When I went to school I studied everything, including *Advaita Vedanta. Vedanta* was my special subject for my masters in philosophy. Very early during my studies I arrived at the conclusion that there is no such thing as mind at all.

There was a well-known professor of psychology at the University of Madras, Dr. Bose. Just a month before my final examinations, I went to him and asked him the question, "We have studied all these six schools of psychology, this, that, and others, exhaustively, but I don't see in all this a place for the 'mind' at all". (At that time I used to say, "Freud is the stupendous fraud of the twentieth century". The fact that he has lasted for a hundred years does not mean anything.) So my problem was that I did not see any mind. So I asked my professor, "Is there a mind?" The only honest fellow that I have met in my life was not any of those holy men but that professor. He said that if I wanted my Master's degree I should not ask such uncomfortable questions. He said, "You would be in trouble. If you want your postgraduate degree, repeat what you have memorized and you will get a degree, if you don't want it, you explore the subject on your own." So I said, "Goodbye". I did not take my examination. I was lucky because at that time I had a lot of money, and I told him that I had four times the income of what he had as professor of psychology. I told him that I could survive with all this money and walked out of the whole business.

But my suspicion [about the mind] persisted for a long time. You see, you cannot be free from all this so easily. You get a feeling, "May be the chap [whoever is talking about the mind] knows what he is talking about. He must have something". Looking back, the whole thing was a stupendous hoax. I told J. Krishnamurti that he was a stupendous hoax of the twentieth century along with Freud. I told him, "You see, you have not freed yourself from this whole idea of messiahs and Theosophy". He could not come out clean from the whole thing.

If you think that he is the greatest teacher of the twentieth century, all right, go ahead, good luck to you. You are not going to have all these transformations, radical or otherwise. Not because I know your future, but because there is nothing there to be transformed, really *nothing*. If you think there is, and think that plum will fall into your stretched palm, good luck to you. What is the point of my telling you?

There is no such thing as enlightenment. So whether Rajneesh is enlightened or some other joker is enlightened is irrelevant. It is you who assumes that somebody is, whoever he is. Good luck to you! Somebody coming and telling me, "That I am" is a big joke. There is nothing to this whole nonsense. I have heard that there is a course in the United States: if you want enlightenment in twenty-four hours they charge you one thousand dollars and if you want it within a week, five hundred dollars, and so on.

Q : Why did you talk about Krishnamurti?

U.G.: It came up, you know. I looked at him, this J.K. freak, sitting here.

Q : It does not seem relevant.

U.G.: What is relevant? Tell me. Are you a Krishnamurti freak or what?

Q : Not exactly.

U.G.: Then it is no problem. What does it matter, whether I discuss the prime minister of India or J. Krishnamurti? You know, I express what I think of that man.

Q : Why don't you keep quiet?

U.G.: Here with all these people around me? Noisy people and noisy things going on around me…?

Q : Can you feel the thoughts of people?

U.G.: Just the way you feel humidity. [Laughter] I cannot decode and translate everything. If I could, you would be in trouble. I am ready to discuss any subject you want. I have opinions on everything from disease to divinity. So I can discuss any subject. In America I always start with health food. That is the obsession there. When you don't have faith in anything, food becomes your obsession in life. So what do we do?

Q : So you say that the mind doesn't exist. What does exist

U.G.: This [pointing to himself] is just a computer.

Q : What difference does it make whether you call it a computer or mind ?

U.G.: If you want to use that word, it is fine by me. The mind is (not that I am giving you a new definition) the totality of man's experiences, thoughts, and feelings. There is no such thing as your mind or my mind. I have no objection if you want to call that totality of man's thoughts, feelings, and experiences by the name 'mind'. But how they are transmitted to us from generation to generation is the question. Is it through the medium of knowledge or is there any other way by which they are transmitted from generation to generation, say for example, through the genes? We don't have the answers yet. Then we come to the idea of memory. What is man? Man is memory. What is that memory? Is it something more than just to remember, to recall a specific thing at a specific time? To all this we have to have some more answers. How do the neurons operate in the brain? Is it all in one area?

The other day I was talking to a neurosurgeon, a very young and bright fellow. He said that memory, or rather the neurons containing memory, are not in one area. The eye, the ear, the nose, all the five sensory organs in your body have a different sort of memory. But they don't yet know for sure. So we have to get more answers. As I see it, everything is genetically controlled. That means you don't have any freedom of action. This is not what we have been taught in India-the fatalistic philosophy. When you say that there is no freedom of action, it means that you have no way of acting except through the help of the knowledge that is passed on to you.

It is in that sense, I said, no action is possible without thought. Any action that is born out of thought which belongs to the totality of knowledge is a protective mechanism. It is protecting itself. It is a self-perpetuating mechanism. You are using it all the time. Every time you experience anything through the help of the knowledge, the knowledge is further strengthened and fortified. So every time you experience greed and condemn it you are adding to its momentum. You are not dealing with the actual greed, anger or desire. You are only interested in using them. Take, for example, desirelessness. You want to be free from desire. But you are not dealing with desire but only with the idea of 'how to be free from desire'.

You are not dealing with something that is living there. Whatever is there or happening there *cannot* be false. You may not like it and may condemn it because it doesn't fit into your social framework. The actions born out of the desire may not fall into the society's framework, which accepts certain actions as socially acceptable, and certain others as anti-social. But you are concerned only about values. You are concerned about grappling with or fighting that which you condemn. Such a concern is born out of culture, society, norms, or whatever. The norms are false and they are falsifying you.

Q : What is the way of making this system, let us say for convenience, 'mind', more efficient?

U.G.: Why, it is already efficient.

Q : We would like it to be more efficient.

U.G.: trying to do that you are only sharpening the instrument. That instrument [thought] is useful in achieving certain results, which are outside the field of living.

Q : Is the mind itself outside the field of living?

U.G.: It is all dead. It can deal with only ideas or thoughts that are actually dead.

Q : Say there are two cities and a river in the middle. These two cities have to communicate, and we have to build a bridge.

U.G.: Yes, you already have the technical know-how.

Q : No. We don't.

U.G.: You don't have, but someone else can give it to you.

Q : Suppose no one gives it.

U.G.: Then, you don't bother about that. We don't discuss hypothetical situations. Who the original man was, how did he get this idea-whether it was by trial and error-we don't bother about all that. The demand to cross over to the other side because there is a rich land there is a kind of drive-the drive for survival. That drive is an extension of this survival mechanism that already exists in nature. You don't have to teach dogs, cats, pigs, and other wild animals, how to search for food, eat and survive. All our activity is nothing but an extension of the same survival mechanism. But in this process we have succeeded in sharpening that instrument. With the help of that instrument we are able to create anything that we are so proud of-progress, this, that, or other.

You may be able to put this record player together and take it apart. This kind of knowledge can be transmitted from one person to another. But the problems that we are interested in solving – the day-to-day problems, living with someone else, or living in this world - are the living problems. They are different every time. We would like to treat them on par with mechanical problems and use that knowledge and experience [coming from dealing with the mechanical problems] to resolve problems of living. But it doesn't seem to work that way. We cannot pass on these experiences to others. It doesn't help. Your own experiences don't always help you. You tell yourself, for example, "If I had this experience ten years ago, my life would have been different". But ten years hence you will be telling yourself exactly the same thing. "If I had this experience ten years ago, ..." But we are now at this point and your past experiences cannot help you to resolve your problems. The learning concerning mechanical problems is useful only in that area and not in any other. But in the area of life we don't learn anything. We simply impose our mechanical knowledge on the coming generations and destroy the possibility of their dealing with their problems in their own way.

The other day I met somebody, a leader. I don't know him. He had come straight from some university. He said, "We have to help the coming generation." He said that the future belongs to the young generation. I told him, "What the hell are you talking about? Why do you want them to prepare to face their future? We have made a mess of the whole thing and they will pay the price. Why is it your problem today? They are more intelligent than us". Our children are more intelligent than us. First of all, we are not ready to face that situation. So we force them into this mould. But it doesn't help them.

The living organism and thought are two different things. Thought cannot conceive of the possibility of anything happening outside the field of time. I don't want to discuss time in a metaphysical sense. I mean by time yesterday, tomorrow, and the day after. The instrument that has produced tremendous results in this area [of time] is unable to solve problems in the area of living. We use this instrument to achieve material results. We also apply the same thing to achieve our so-called spiritual goals. It works here but it doesn't work there. Whether it is materialistic goals or spiritual goals, the instrument we are using is matter. Therefore, the so-called spiritual goals are also materialistic in their value and in their results. I don't see any difference between the two. I haven't found any spirit there. The whole structure, which we have built on the foundation of the assumed 'self' or 'spirit', therefore, collapses.

What is mind? You can give a hundred definitions. It is just a simple mechanical functioning. The body is responding to stimuli. It is only a stimulus-responding mechanism. It does not know of any other action. But through the translation of stimulus in terms of human values, we have destroyed the sensitivity of the living organism. You may talk of the sensitivity of the mind and the sensitivity of your feelings towards your fellow beings. But it doesn't mean a thing.

Q: But there must be some sensitivity without the stimulus.

U.G.: What I am talking about is the sensitivity of sensory perceptions. But what you are concerned with is sensuality. They are different things. The sensory activity of the living organism is all that exists. Culture has superimposed on it something else that is always in the field of sensuality. Whether it is a spiritual experience or any other experience, it is in the field of pleasure. So the demand for permanence is really the problem. The moment a sensation is translated as a pleasurable one there is already a problem. The translation is possible only through the help of knowledge. But the body rejects both pain and pleasure for the simple reason that any sensation that lasts longer than its natural duration is destroying the sensitivity of the nervous system. But we are interested only in the sensual aspects of the sensory activity.

Q : When you refer to 'we' whom do you mean?

U.G.: Because we are using the word 'we', you are asking me the questions, "Who is the 'we'?" "What is the entity that is using it?" etc. This is only a self-perpetuating mechanism, and it is maintaining its continuity. When I say 'self', I don't mean the 'self' in the sense in which we normally use the word. It is more like a self-starter in a car. It is perpetuating itself through this repetitive process.

Q : What is an example of sensitivity?

U.G.: There is no sensitivity other then the sensitive nervous system responding to stimuli. So, if you are concerned or preoccupied with the sensitivity of anything else, you are blurring the sensory activity. The eyes cannot see, but the moment you see , the translation of sensory perception comes into operation. There is always a space between perception and memory. Memory is like sound. Sound is very slow, whereas light travels faster. All these sensory activities or perceptions are like light. They are very fast. But for some reason we have lost the capacity to kick that [memory] into the background and allow these things to move as fast as they occur in nature. Thought comes, captures it [the sensory perception], and says that it is this or that. That is what you call recognition, or naming, or whatever you want to call it. The moment you recognize this as the tape recorder, the name 'tape recorder' also is there. So recognition and naming are not two different things. We would like to create a space between them and believe that these two are different things. As I said earlier, the physical eye by itself has no way of translating the physical perception into the framework of your knowledge.

Q : Can this naming be postponed for sometime?

U.G.: What do you want to postpone it for? What do you want to achieve by that? I am describing the functioning of sensory perception. Physiologists talk about this as a response to a stimulus. But the fact that this particular response is for that particular stimulus is something that cannot be experienced by you. It is one unitary movement. Response cannot be separated from the stimulus. It is because they are inseparable that we can do nothing to prevent the possibility of the knowledge about past experiences coming into operation before the sensory perceptions move from one thing to another.

Q : Why do you use a vague word like 'mind'? All that we are referring to is the brain like any other organ of the body. Why should we create another word?

U.G.: Because it has become a bugbear for many people "peace of mind", "control of mind", etc.

Q : You first create the mind and then start pouring it out.

U.G.: We invent what is called a thoughtless state or an effortless state, I don't know for what reason. Why one should be in an effortless state is beyond me. But to be in an effortless state or to act effortlessly we use effort. That's absurd. We don't seem to have any way of putting ourselves into a thoughtless state except through thought.

Q : Do you mean to say that the word is the thing?

U.G.: It makes no difference. I don't want to indulge in this frivolity that the word is not the thing. If the word is not the thing what the hell is it? Without the word you are not separate from whatever you are looking at or what is going on inside of you. The word is the knowledge. Without the knowledge you don't even know whether it is pain or pleasure that you experience, whether it is happiness or unhappiness, whether it is boredom or its opposite. We really don't know what is going on there. Using the expression, "What is going on there" itself implies that you already have captured that within the framework of your experiencing structure and distorted it.

Q : Sir, is not the word a super imposition on the comprehension of a thing?

U.G.: Is there any comprehension?

Q : Suppose I comprehend, and then there is a word – 'U. G. Krishnamurti'. First I comprehend and then there is a superimposition through a word.

U.G.: What do you mean? You have to explain. That is too difficult a word for me-'comprehend'. You can produce a simpler word for me. I am not with you.

Q : If my eyes take you in comprehending...

U.G.: Then, what you are saying is something, which cannot be experienced by you.

Q : No. It is not for the purpose of being liberated or controlled. It just happens.

U.G.: You can't even assert that it just happens. There are no two things there. As far as the eye is concerned it does not even know that it is looking.

Q : I cannot decide what I am going to see.

U.G.: You are not the one that is operating the camera. The thoughts, which we are talking about, don't originate there. No action of yours is self-generated. The problem is really with the language. We can manage with three hundred basic words.

Q : Even less...

U.G.: Even less. Children can express all emotions. If they can't use words, they are still able to express their emotions so beautifully, in simple ways. Their whole bodies express their joy, each in a different way. But we are proud of the words we use because for us they are instruments of power. For us knowledge is power. "I know, and you don't know". That gives you power. There is no such thing as knowledge for knowledge's sake. It is good to write an essay on knowledge for knowledge's sake or art for the sake of art. Is their beauty? What is beauty? Only when it is framed, you call it beauty. It is thought that has framed something, the nature of which we really don't know. To use your word, there is no way of comprehending. We don't even know what is going on there.

Q : Or when the experience is over....

U.G.: No, no. That line I am very familiar with [Laughs]; "While you are experiencing the thing you are not aware of it". That is a copybook maxim. But that's not true.

Q : You know when you use the phrase 'not true'....

U.G.: What do you want me to say?

Q : There has to be something on the basis of which you judge that this is not true. That is where the difficulty starts...

U.G.: It is not a value judgement. 'Nice', 'horrible', 'detestable' - we have plenty of these words. There is no need for a verb. It is the verb that creates a problem. For purpose of communication we have to rely upon words. But when I say, "He is a nasty fellow", it is not a value judgement but a descriptive sentence. That is the way you describe or fit the actions of that individual into the framework of nastiness. I have to use that word, but it is not a value judgement in my case. Not that I am placing myself on a higher or superior level. "What is the good man good for?" - I don't know. Maybe for society a good man is a useful citizen, and for bad man a good man is good because he can exploit him. But as far as I am concerned what a good man is good for I wouldn't know. The problem with language is, no matter how we try to express ourselves; we are caught up in the structure of words. There is no point in creating a new language, new lingo to express anything. There is nothing there to be expressed except to free yourself from the stranglehold of thought. And there is nothing that you can do to free yourself either through any volition of yours or through any effort of yours.

Q : But we have to understand.

U.G.: What is there is to understand? To understand anything we have to use the same instrument that is used to understand this mechanical computer that is there before me. Its working can be understood through repeatedly trying to learn to operate it. You try again and again. If it doesn't work, there is someone who can tell you how to operate it, take it apart and put it together. You yourself will learn through a repetitive process - how to change this, improve this, modify this, and so on and so forth. This instrument [thought], which we have been using to understand, has not helped us to understand anything except that every time you are using it you are sharpening it. Someone asked me, "What is philosophy? How does it help me to live in this day-today existence?" It doesn't help you in any way except that it sharpens the instrument of the intellect. It doesn't in any way help you to understand life.

If that [thought] is not the instrument, and if there is no other instrument, then is there anything to understand? 'Intuitive perception' or 'intuitive understanding' is only a product of the same instrument. The understanding, that there is nothing to understand, nothing to get, somehow dawned on me. I seriously wanted to understand. Otherwise I would not waste forty-nine years of my life. But when once this understanding that there is nothing to understand somehow dawned on me, the very demand to be free from anything, even from the physical demands, was not there any more. But how this happened to me I really wouldn't know. So there is no way I can share this with you, because it is not in the area of experiencing things.

Q : How do you place those people who don't have this burden of trying to understand life but are just living in the world? How do you place them?

U.G.: Whether you are interested in *moksha*, liberation, freedom, transformation, you name it, or you are interested in happiness without one moment of unhappiness, pleasure without pain, it's the same thing. Whether one is here in India or in Russia or in America or anywhere, what people want is to have one [happiness] without the other [unhappiness]. But there is no way you can have one without the other. This demand is not in the interest of the survival of this living organism. There is an extraordinarily alert, and alacritous quality to it [the organism]. The body is rejecting all sensations. Sensations have a limited life; beyond a particular duration the body cannot take them. It is either throwing them out or absorbing them. Otherwise they destroy the body. The eyes are interested in seeing things but not as beauty; the ears hear things but not as music.

The body does not reject a noise because it is the barking of a dog or braying of an ass. It just responds to the sound. If you call it a response to the sound, then we get into trouble. So you don't even know that it is a sound. Anything that is harsh, anything that would destroy the sensitivity of the nervous system, the body cuts out. It is like a thermostat. To some extent the body has a way of saving itself from heat, cold, or anything that is inimical to it. It takes care of itself for a short period, and then thought helps you to take the next step to cover yourself, or to move yourself away from the dangerous situation you find yourself in. you will naturally move away from the cement mixer that is making a loud noise and is destroying the sensitivity of your nervous system. The fear that you would be destroyed because the sound is bad, or that you will become a nervous wreck, and so on and so forth, is part of your paranoia.

Q : Sir, is there is a state in which you just receive without reacting?

U.G.: There is only reaction and you are reacting. If the reaction is not there, it is a different matter. Unfortunately, it seems to be there all the time. That is why you are asking the question. But response that I am talking about is something that cannot be experienced by you at all. If I say that the response to a stimulus is spontaneous and that it is a pure action, then that action is no action at all in any ordinary sense of the word. It is one unitary movement. It [the response] cannot be separated [from the stimulus]. The moment you separate them [the stimulus and the response] and say that this is the response to that stimulus; you have brought the element of reaction into the picture already. Let us not fool ourselves that there is a spontaneous action, pure action, and all that kind of nonsense.

Q : I have two questions, Sir. One, assuming that a cat has a computer, though a smaller one, and I have a bigger one, what else is the basic difference...

U.G.: Your computer is more complex and complicated. Evolution implies the simple becoming complex. They say that the brainpower of all the ants in an anthill is much more than the brainpower of a human being. Whether that is there in the human body is the result of what has been passed on from one species to another. We use thought not only for our self-aggrandizement but we also use it to destroy, for no reason, other species of life around us. Physical fear is totally different from the fear of losing what you have, the fear of not getting what you want. You can call it physiological fear.

So, the simple becomes complex. We don't even know if there is any such thing as evolution. We rule out spiritual evolution. Those who assumed that there is such a thing as spirit or soul or center, or whatever you want to call it, say that it also goes through the evolutionary process and perfects itself. And for that you have to take one birth after another. I don't know how many births there may be, 84 million, or god knows what the figure is.

Q : Coming back to the question that a cat has a smaller computer and I have a more complex computer...

U.G.: Basically, they both operate in exactly the same way.

Q : Looking from the cat's point of view now...

U.G.: I don't know how the cat looks at it. The cat can look at the king, whoever told the story, but we dare not look at the king, you see [laughter].

Q : Don't put up those restrictions yourself...

U.G.: I don't know. It is an assumption on our part like any other assumption or speculation about how the cat looks. I say sometimes that when I look at something, it is like a cat or a dog looking at things...

Q : What is the difference?

U.G.: I don't see any difference.

Q : There is none?

U.G.: There is none.

Q : There isn't any difference except the differences we create. Then we get into them.

U.G.: That's what I am saying.

Q : Yes, I agree with you.

U.G.: I don't know for sure how a cat looks at me. Outwardly, the cat looks at me and I look at the cat or at anything else the same way. There is not even looking, you see, if it comes to that. Is there a looking without a looker? I don't use those words in a metaphysical sense. Is there any seeing without a seer? There is no seeing even. 'What is going on?' – the very question is absurd. We want to know everything, and that is our problem.

Q : You must create a problem to solve it.

U.G.: Yes, but you can survive without that knowing.

Q : That is what I was coming to...

U.G.: We can survive. All the species have survived for millions of years, and we have evolved out of them. Without them probably we wouldn't be here today. So why this demand to know?

Q : To know what?

U.G.: To know that you are happy, that you are bored, that you are not free, that you are enlightened or not enlightened, that you cannot have pleasure all the time - the whole lot. Even the demand to know, "How did you stumble into this?" is the same. You want to know the cause. You want to know what I did or what I did not do. You see you are trying to establish a cause-and-effect relationship between the two. You do this for the simple reason that you want 'that' to happen to you.

Your background is completely and totally different from my background. Somebody was saying that my background, my life story is very dramatic. But your background is equally dramatic. The impossibility of what is there to express itself is really the problem. What it is that is making it impossible? What prevents the uniqueness, which is the end product of millions and millions of years [of evolution], to express itself? It [the mind] is just two thousand years old. It is too silly to think that it is going to succeed. It is not going to succeed. You don't go about calling yourself unique. I don't go around the world telling everyone that I am a unique man. No, not in that sense. But you *are* unique. The two uniques don't even bother to compare how unique they are. I have to use that word uniqueness because it *is* really unique. Even two human bodies are not the same. Now they [the scientists] have come to that conclusion. Unfortunately, all that understanding is the result of the research and experiments in crime laboratories to track down the culprits through their fingerprints. Not only through prints, but they can track down a man from the smell, or a teeny-weeny bit of his hair. [Laughter] Your saliva is different, your tissues are different, and your semen is different from everyone else's. No two faces are the same.

I studied botany in the university. When you study the leaves under a microscope, you can see that no two leaves are the same. Our whole attempt, for idiotic reasons, to fit every individual into a common mould is not going to succeed. If we push it too hard, we will probably blow ourselves up. That is inevitable because we have in our possession tremendous instruments of destruction, far surpassing the capacity of the so-called mind to deal with them.

Q : I want to return to my question. When I started I said there are two computers, X and Y. Their computers have been programmed. Everything is programmed. Once everything is programmed, everything - effort, will, and all that - is immaterial.

U.G.: Yes, that's what I am saying.

Q : There is no scope for the word called 'effort'...

U.G.: That's what I say too...Or for freedom of action.

Q : ...will or any such thing. Because everything is programmed.

U.G.: Yes, not only by culture, but also by nature itself, probably for its own survival. We don't know; it [each species] is programmed. That is why I say that there is no freedom of action at all. The demand for freedom of action is meaningless.

Q : Well, maybe it is also programmed, and that is why people keep on demanding. We can leave the matter at that. To come back to the cat and man, personally, I think, there is absolutely no difference.

U.G.: No. If we had remained that way, probably we would have become a different species. This is only a speculation.

Q : Every time we get into ice age, or another age when the hole thing restarts, you start from that level.

U.G.: Yes, we have come to nuclear age where the future is very gloomy. Anyway that is not the point.

Q : You know, gloomy may be another way of describing...

U.G.: If the human race goes we also go with it.

Q : All the computers will be destroyed.

U.G.: Not only the computers, everything will be destroyed.

Q : No, computers, because I have reduced everything to computers... My second question: You said you must be highly obliged to all the spiritual teachers at least for one reason, namely, but for them I or you or anyone would not have realized that there is no such thing as enlightenment.

U.G.: I am not with you. Say that again.

Q : ...because they have been selling enlightenment asa product and we go after it.

U.G.: And then you discover that it is a shoddy piece of goods that they are selling.

Q : Right. But for them you would not have realized even this.

U.G.: I don't think that there is room for any gratitude to them.

Q : No. I wouldn't say that.

U.G.: See, you are thrown into a situation from where you have no escape. You are trapped in it. The very attempt on your part to 'untrap' (is there any such word?) or free yourself, or get out of that trap, is making you sink further into it. What we are left with is total helplessness to do anything. But yet, unfortunately, we have a hope that there is something we can do, we don't stop at that total helplessness; we go on and on until the dead-end. The living teachers and yet unborn ones are hammering into our heads that they have answers for our problems and that they have the means to save the whole situation.

Q : Since there are no questions, there is no question ofanswers. Where are the questions?

U.G.: All the questions are born out of the answers. But nobody wants the answers. The end of the questions is the end of the answers. The end of the solution is the end of the problem. We are only dealing with solutions and not with the problems.

Actually there are no problems; there are only solutions. But we don't even have the guts to say that they don't work. Even if you have discovered that they don't work, sentimentality comes into the picture. The feeling, "That man in whom I have placed my confidence and belief cannot con himself and con everyone else", comes in the way of throwing the whole thing out of the window, down the drain. The solutions are still a problem. Actually there is no problem there. The only problem is to find out the inadequacy or uselessness of all the solutions that have been offered to us. The questions naturally are born out of the assumptions and answers that we have taken for granted as real answers. But we really don't want any answers to the questions, because an answer to the question is the end of the answer. If one answer ends, all the other answers also go. You don't have to deal with ten different answers. You deal with one question and that puts an end to the answer. Yet I have to accept the reality of the world as it is imposed on me for purposes of functioning sanely.

Q : Will it not lead us to the tribal level again?

U.G.: We have not moved away from the tribal level. [Laughter] Have we really? The cave man didn't have the means to blow up the whole world, but we do. And animals don't kill anybody for an idea or belief. Only we do it.

Q : Is there, Sir, any evolution apart from the biological one?

U.G.: You mean spiritual?

Q : Well, any other.

U.G.: Even the biological evolution, we don't know for sure. Some idlers like me have observed certain things and they have arrived at some conclusions.

Q : Please tell us.

U.G.: I am an illiterate. I don't read much. I haven't read anything for ages now.

Q : For idling you don't need literacy, Sir! [Laughter]

U.G.: I don't even observe. At least the scientists have this motivation, if I may use that word, to observe things and understand the laws of nature.

Q : It's all a self-centered activity.

U.G.: It's all a self-centered activity. It is a question of self-fulfillment. You may feel that I am fulfilling myself through this talk, surrounding myself with all the people here. Yes, you can throw that at me and maybe there is something to it. I really don't know. Pleasure it is not. I have pain here- [laughter] -a headache.

Q : Acute pain leads to pleasure.

U.G.: They are the same, Sir. We forget that. Pain indicates a healing process in the body. That is what I have discovered. We don't give the body a chance to recover but rush to the doctor.

Q : Actually all these spiritual leaders...

U.G.: They don't exist without us, Sir.

Q : No, they don't. They have confused mankind to such an extent...

U.G.: They can't confuse us. We want to be confused. Otherwise how can they confuse us? We are willing victims in this matter.

Q : We are fooling ourselves.

U.G.: Yes, we are fools. If one fool leaves, there are ten fools to change places with him. There will never by any shortage of fools at any time.

Q : Sir , again we are coming to the same point. The enlightened ones...

U.G.: Have you come across one except the claimants?

Q : We have come across the one who is sitting before us, Sir. [Referring to U.G.] [Laughter]

U.G.: No, no. Let's not indulge in that sort of thing. You will have no use for it. You cannot fit me into a value system at all. A value system has no use for me, and there is no question of my setting up a holy business. I have no way of telling myself that I am different from you. As I said, you have to take my word for it. If you still say, "No, we don't accept it", it is just fine with me. What can I do?

Q : But the understanding of their thought processes and all those things, which you have come across, can help us.

U.G.: I didn't understand a thing. I am telling you. There is no process to go through to reach anywhere. It looks like I went through some process. No. I did not. I wasted so many years of my life in pursuit of the goals that I had set for myself. If it had dawned on me during the early stages of my life that there is nothing to understand, I wouldn't have wasted forty-nine years of my life and denied myself everything. I was born with a silver spoon, sleeping on a luxurious bed. Do you think if I had known all this I would go there and lie down in a cave repeating things that I did not know? I was repeating things and reading books that I did not understand when I was fourteen. It is too silly. Looking back I would say I wasted all that time. But anyway I don't see any way of comparing what I did with what I stumbled into. I have no way of saying, "This is it", and then "I was like that" There is no point [of reference] here. Since there is no point here, there is no way I can look back and say *that* was the point.

You may very well ask me the question, "How come you are saying that despite all you did you have stumbled into whatever you have stumbled into?" But I have to put it that way – "despite", "in spite of" – or whatever words you want to use. All that did not lead me to this. "How do you know that it did not lead you there?" you might ask. What I went through is not part of that knowing mechanism. "Why do you say that it is a state of not-knowing?" you can ask. "How can you talk of that state of not-knowing in terms of the known?" you may ask. You are only pushing me to give an answer. To answer your question, your demand, your persistence to know what that state is, I say that it is a state of not knowing; not that there is something which cannot be known. I am not talking of the unknowable, the inexpressible, and the inexperienceable.

I am not talking of any of those things. That still keeps the movement going. What there is is only the known. There is no such thing, for instance, as the fear of the unknown. You can't be afraid of the unknown, because the unknown, as you say, is *unknown*. The fear that you are talking about is the fear of the known coming to an end. That seems to be the problem. When I use this phrase-'the state of unknowing'- it is not a synonymous term for transformation, *moksha*, liberation, God-realization, self-realization, and what have you.

Q : When I visited a place where people who are mentally different are kept…

U.G.: Mentally different or sick or ill or…

Q : I would prefer to call them mentally different because they think we are mentally different and vice versa.

U.G.: That is true.

Q : The dividing line is very thin. They may be looking at us as victims. Really we don't know who is different. But biologically both of us are functioning.

U.G.: …exactly the same way.

Q : ...the same way. What could be the basis for calling them mentally different?

U.G.: Because we have established the so-called normal man.

Q : That's what I am hinting at.

U.G.: Some people who are in the All India Institute of Mental Health at Bangalore visited me. One of them is a top neurosurgeon. I asked him the same question, "Who is normal? Who is sane and who is insane?" He said, "Statistically speaking, we are sane". That was quite satisfactory to me. And then I asked him, "Why are you putting all of them there and treating them? How much help do you give them?" He said, "Not even two percent of them are helped. We send them back to their homes, but they keep coming back". "Then why are you running this show?" I asked him. He said, "The government pays the money and the families don't want to keep those people in their homes".

So, we now move on from there to the basic question, "Who is sane and who is insane?" I have lots of them coming to see me. Even this Institute sometimes sends people to me. Even people who are hardcore cases come to me. But the line of demarcation between them and me is very thin. The difference seems to be that they have given up, whereas I am not in conflict with the society. I take it. That's all the difference. There is nothing that prevents me from fitting into the framework of society. I am not in conflict with the society. When once you are, I don't like to use the word, freed from, or are not trapped in, this duality of right and wrong, good and bad, you can never do anything bad. As long as you are caught up in wanting to do only good, you will always do bad. Because the 'good' you seek is only in the future. You will be good some other time and until then you remain a bad person. So, the so-called insane have given up, and we are doing them the greatest harm and disservice by pushing them to fit themselves into this framework of ours which is rotten. [Laughter] I don't just say it is rotten, but it is.

I don't fight society. I am not in conflict with it. I am not even interested in changing it. The demand to bring about a change in myself isn't there any more. So, the demand to change this framework or the world at large isn't there. It is not that I am indifferent to the suffering man. I suffer with the suffering man and am happy with the happy man. You seem to get pleasure out of the suffering of somebody. But why don't you get the same pleasure when you see a rich man throwing his weight around? They are the same. This you call pleasure and that you call jealousy or envy. But I don't see any difference between the two. I see suffering. Individually, there isn't anything that I can do. And at the same time I don't want to use this [suffering] for my self-aggrandizement, my self-fulfillment. The problem is there, and we are individually responsible for it. Yet we don't want to accept the responsibility for creating the problems. The problems are not created by nature. It is we who have created the problems. There is plenty, there is bounty in nature; but we take away what rightfully belongs to everybody and then say that you should give charity. That's too absurd!

The practice of charity, started by the religious men, is what refuses to deal with the problems squarely. I may give something to a poor man because he is suffering. But unless I have something more than he has, there is no way I can help. What do I do if I don't have the means to help him? What do I do in a situation where I am totally helpless? That helplessness only makes me sit with him and cry.

What Is The Meaning Of Life?

Q : I have read a statement that is attributed to you. It says that nature is not interested in creating a perfect be ing, but that its interest is only to create a perfect species. What do you mean by that?

U.G.: We have for centuries been made to believe that the end product of human evolution, if there is one, is the creation of perfect beings modeled after the great spiritual teachers of mankind and their behaviour patterns.

Q : By great spiritual teachers you mean people like Jesus and the Buddha?

U.G.: All of them. All the great teachers: the occidental, the oriental, and the Chinese teachers. That is the basic problem we are confronted with. I don't think I have any special insights into the laws of nature. But if there is any thing as an end product of human evolution (I don't know if there is such a thing as evolution, but we take it for granted that there is), what nature is trying to produce is not a perfect being.

Q : But scientific research has revealed that there is such a thing as evolution.

U.G.: Even today some universities don't allow their students to study Darwin's *Origin of Species.* His statements have been proved to be wrong to some extent because he said that acquired characteristics couldn't be transmitted to the succeeding generations. But every time they [the scientists] discover something new they change their theories.

Nature does not use anything as a model. It is interested in perfecting the species. It is trying to create perfect species and not perfect beings. We are not ready to accept that. What nature has created in the form of human species is something extraordinary. It is an unparalleled creation. But culture is interested in fitting the actions of all human beings into a common mould. That is because it is interested in maintaining the status quo, its value system. That is where the real conflict is. This [referring to himself] is something that cannot be fitted into that value system.

Q : I have been in touch with your statements over the years. You can be called a universal pessimist. Given your position, I am tempted to ask, "Why don't you commit suicide?" I cannot deny that you are also a very lively person.

U.G.: Since I have not come into the world of my own choice, I don't think I will opt for suicide. It is not a clever statement that I am making, but these labels that I am a pessimist and others are optimists do not really mean anything. They have put me into the framework of a pessimist, a nihilist, an atheist, and many others. How can you, for instance, call me a godman when I sometimes go to the extent of saying that God is irrelevant?

If I make a statement like that, I don't mean that I am questioning the existence of God. The theologians discussing everlastingly, trying to impress upon us through their dialectical thinking, the cosmological, ontological, and teleological proofs of the existence of God, do not impress me. We are not concerned with that question at all. It has become irrelevant to us because we use that to exploit others. We use thinking as an instrument of destruction. We want to believe that God is on our side. During the last world war, the Germans claimed that God was their copilot, and the British also claimed that God was their copilot. Both of them destroyed life and property. So we would like God to be on our side all the time and use Him. But what has come out of that is only violence. Belief in God, or belief in anything, separates us from others. When we find that we cannot force our beliefs on others we resort to violence. We would like everybody to believe the same thing. When we fail in that attempt of ours to make everybody believe in God, or no God, or even our political systems-the right or the left- what is left is only violence.

Q : I began with this whole question of nature because what I find in your statement is a profound sense of nature, a profound sense of the absolute and primitive reality of life itself, which seems to me an extraordinarily positive force and a force for the good.

U.G.: The fundamental mistake that humanity made somewhere along the line, is, or was, or whatever is the correct verb [chuckles], to experience this separateness from the totality of life. At that time there occurred in man, which includes woman also, this self-consciousness that separated him from the life around. He was so isolated that it frightened him. The demand to be a part of the totality of life around him created this tremendous demand for the ultimate. He thought that the spiritual goals of God, truth, or reality, would help him to become part of the 'whole' again. But the very attempt on his part to become one with or become integrated with the totality of life has kept him only more separate. Isolated functioning is not part of nature. But this isolation has created a demand for finding out ways and means of becoming a part of nature. But thought in its very nature can only create problems and cannot help us solve them.

We don't seem to realize that it is thought that is separating us from the totality of things. The belief that this is the one that can help us to keep in tune with the totality is not going to materialize. So, it has come up with all kinds of ingenuous, if I may use that word, ideas of insight and intuition.

Q : There are a lot of words.

U.G.: Yes, we have a plethora of words. You know it is said that Shakespeare, that great playwright and poet, had a vocabulary of only four thousand words. I don't know if that is true. But now we have many thousands of words. We come up with every kind of phrase to cover up this impossibility of trying to use words to understand the reality of things. That is where the real problem is. Thought has not succeeded so far in understanding reality, but that [thought] is all that we are left with. We cannot question thought. We cannot brush it aside. We know in a way that it cannot help us, but can only create problems. We are not ready to throw it out and find out if there is any other way, if there is any answer.

Q : One of the things that strike me as you speak is howin many ways what you say is related to the underlying philosophy of Hinduism. I mean Hinduism that speaks of theoriginal unity of all things.

U.G.: I am not for a moment expounding Hinduism here or in India. In fact, they think that I am not a Hindu. Yet the Hindus are ready to accept [to some degree] what I am saying. They say, "What you are saying seems to be true, but the way you are putting things is not acceptable". They brush me aside. But at the same time they cannot totally brush me aside. They always try to fit me into their framework or reference point. If they cannot do that, the whole tradition in which they have a tremendous investment is at stake. So they necessarily have to try to fit me into that framework. So far. nobody has succeeded. Many philosophers in India have been asked about my statements, and they know that they can very well deal with any philosophy, any thinker, past and present, but they have some difficulty in fitting me into any particular frame that they know of. What they say is, and I quote, "There is no way we can fit this man into any known cage. So what we have to do is to let the bird fly".

Q : I suppose that the 'free flying' fits in perfectly with primitive nature.

U.G.: You know what the word 'religion' means?

Q : It is to be tied down in some way.

U.G.: I am not interested in the root meaning of the words at all, but it means "to connect you back to source".

Q : Yes.

U.G.: On the other hand, religion has created schisms. It has been responsible for tremendous destruction of life and property. It is very unfortunate. But, nevertheless, the fact does remain that religion has failed in its purpose.

We live in the hope and die in the hope that somehow the very same thing that has failed us will one day rescue us. You cannot conceive of the impossibility of creating a harmony between humans and the life around through thought.

Q : Although religion has no doubt done many destructive things, it has also done many creative things. I mean great art and literature, Shakespeare himself, in a way, was coming out of basically a religious experience. Certainly that is true of the Western civilization, which arises out of the Christian experience.

U.G.: That's true. That is why when a void is created, when all the systems have failed, there is the danger of a demand for the religious stuff stepping into it and trying to tell us, "We have the answers to your problems". But the revolutions have failed. I am not against any value system, but the demand to fit ourselves into it [a value system] is the cause of man's suffering.

Q : Where then do we go from here? I am not going to ask you what is the purpose of life, because obviously, as you were saying, that is really not a relevant question.

U.G.: No, it is a relevant question, but is born out of the assumption that we know about life. Nobody knows anything about life. We have only concepts, ideations, and mentations about life. Even the scientists who are trying to understand life and its origin come up only with theories and definitions of life. You may not agree with me, but all thought, all thinking is dead. Thinking is born out of dead ideas. Thought or the thinking mechanism trying to touch life, experience it, capture, and give expression to it are impossible tasks.

What we are concerned about is living. Living is our relationship with our fellow beings, with the life around. When we have everything that we can reasonably ask for, all the material comforts that you have in the West, the question naturally arises: "Is that all?" The moment you pose that question to yourself, we have created a problem. If that's all there is, what then is the next step to take? We do not see any meaning in our life, and so we pose this question to ourselves, and throw this question at all those who you think have the answers.

What is the meaning of life? What is the purpose of life? It may have its own meaning, it may have its own purpose. By understanding the meaning of life and the purpose of life we are not going to improve, change, modify, or alter our behaviour patterns in any way. But there is a hope that by understanding the meaning of life, we can bring about a change. There may not be any meaning of life. If it has a meaning, it is already in operation there. Wanting to understand the meaning of life seems to be a futile attempt on our part. We go on asking these questions.

Once a very old gentleman, ninety-five years old, who was considered to be a great spiritual man and who taught the great scriptures all the time to his followers, came to see me. He asked me two questions. He asked me, "What is the meaning of life? I have written hundreds of books telling people all about the meaning and purpose of life, quoting all the scriptures and interpreting them. I haven't understood the meaning of life. You are the one who can give an answer to me". I told him, "Look, you are ninety-five years old and you haven't understood the meaning of life. When are you going to understand the meaning of life? There may not be any meaning to life at all". The next question he asked me was, "I have lived ninety-five years and I am going to die one of these days. I want to know what will happen after my death". I said, "You may not live long to know anything about death. You have to die now. Are you ready to die?" As long as you are asking the question, "What is death?" or "What is there after death?" you are already dead. These are all dead questions. A living man would never ask those questions.

Q : Let us ask then another question, which is not intellectual. What should we do?

U.G.: [Laughs] We have been for centuries told what to do. Why are we asking the same question, "What to do?" What to do in relation to what? What I am emphasizing is that the demand to bring about a change in ourselves is the cause of our suffering. I may say that there is nothing to be changed. But the revolutionary teachers come and tell us that there is something there in which you have to bring about a radical revolution. Then we assume there is such a thing as soul, spirit, or the 'I'. What I assert all the time is that I haven't found anything like the self or soul there.

This question haunted me all my life, and suddenly it hit me: "There is no self to realize. What the hell have I been doing all this time?" You see, that hits you like a lightning. Once that hits you, the whole mechanism of the body that is controlled by this thought [of the 'I'] is shattered. What is left is the tremendous living organism with an intelligence of its own. What you are left with is the pulse, the beat, and the throb of life.

"There must be something more, and we have to do something to become part of the whole thing". Such demands have arisen because of our assumption that we have been created for a grander purpose than that for which other species on this planet have been created. That's the fundamental mistake we have made. Culture is responsible for our assuming this. We thus come to believe that the whole creation is for the benefit of man. The demand to use nature for our purposes has created all the ecological problems. It is not such an easy thing for us to deal with these problems. We have reached a point where there is no going back. You may say that I am a pessimist again.

The point is, we have probably arrived at a place where there is no going back. What is the fate of mankind and what is one to do? Anything that is born out of thought is destructive in its nature. That is why I very often say in my conversations and interviews that thought, in its birth, in its nature, in its expression, and in its action, is fascist. Thought is interested in protecting itself, and is always creating frontiers around itself. And it wants to protect the frontiers. That is why we create frontiers around us: our families, our nations, and then this planet.

Q : I am fascinated because this is one of the most consistently intellectual conversations I have had in a long time.

U.G.: [Laughs] Whatever else I may or may not have been, I have never been an intellectual. People ask me questions, and I say that I am an illiterate.

Q : Well, your logic is absolutely consistent. The consistency of your position is unassailable. It would seem to me that the best thing to do in some way is what some of the Christian mystics did. They said that God is nothing.

U.G.: Remarkable people.

Q: That leads them to a silence almost to the end. Why do you speak? I pose the question to you.

U.G.: Why do I speak?

Q: Yes.

U.G.: Why do I speak? [Laughter] Am I speaking? You know, it may sound very funny to you. I have nothing to say, and what I am saying is not born out of my thinking. You may not accept this. But it is not a logical ascertained premise that I am putting across. It may sound very funny to you, and you have put me in a very precarious position by asking me why I am talking. Am I talking? Really I am not, you see. There is nobody who is talking here. I use this simile of a ventriloquist. He is actually carrying on both sides of the dialogue, but we attribute one side of it to the dummy in front of him. In exactly the same way, all your questions are born out of the answers you already have. Any answer anybody gives should put an end to your questions. But it does not. And we are not ready to accept the fact that all the questions are born out of the answers. If the questions go, the answers we take for granted also go with them. But we are not ready to throw the answers away, because sentiments come into the picture. The tremendous investments we have made, and the faith we have in the teachers, are also at stake. Therefore, we are not ready to brush aside the answers.

Actually we do not want answers for our questions. The assumption that the questions are different from the questioner is also false. If the answer goes, the questioner also goes. The questioner is nothing but the answers. That is really the problem.

We are not ready to accept this answer because it will put an end to the answers that we have accepted for ages as the real answers.

Q : And so, we keep asking questions.

U.G.: Yes, asking questions.

Q : And where would we have been without a few questions to ask? [Laughter]

U.G.: You have asked the questions and I have tried to give the answers.

Q : Do you say that we are two separate people or just part of the universal life force?

U.G.: There is no way I can separate myself except when I use the knowledge that is common to us both. So there is no way I can create this individual here [pointing to himself] and experience that there is such a thing as a human body here, that there is something that is talking here. There is nobody who is talking. It is just a computer. And, you are interested in operating the computer. Whatever is coming out of me that you think is the answer is a printout.

What I am trying to say is that I have no image of myself. I have no way I can create the image. The only instruments I have are my sensory perceptions. My sensory perceptions function independently of each other. There is no coordinator who is coordinating all the sensory perceptions and creating an image.

Since I have no way I can create an image here within me, I have no way of creating an image of you and put you up there.

But it does not mean that I am this microphone, or you, or that table. It is not that I am the table, or the microphone, or this glass of water, or this visitor's card; not at all. There is no way, however, that I can separate myself from any of these except through the help of the knowledge, which is our common property. The questions get answered through that knowledge. That is also the only way I can experience things.

Actually, what we see here [in ourselves] is the opposite of what we would like to be, what we would want to be, what we think ought to be or should be. Otherwise there is no way you can create an image of yourself. Since you want to be something other than what you are, (that's what the culture has put in there,) you create something that is the opposite [of what you would like to be]. That is all the time struggling to be something other than what it is. So what is here is the opposite of what you would like to be, and so that creates time. Thought can never conceive the possibility of achieving anything except in time. It does not want to let go of this image that is created by what you would like to be, what you think you ought to be or should be. That's really the problem.

"What is going on here are two persons exchanging ideas"- this I really don't know. I have no way of experiencing that at all. But if you ask me the question, "What is it that is talking?" I say it is U.G. and you. It may take a little time because the computer has to come up with the information that is there. I mean not in a simple case like this but in more complex cases.

We think that our memory is very fast. But actually it is slower than the activity of the sensory perceptions. There is an illusion that memory is operating all the time, trying to capture everything within its framework. But the illusion is created by the mind in order to maintain the continuity of our identity. We can't afford to let go of our identity whether we are asleep, awake or dreaming. This identity is there all the time, and we do not want to let go of it.

I am not saying that thought is useless or any such thing. Its interest is to maintain its continuity. When the identity is not there, you have no way of identifying yourself with anything except through the help of knowledge. So, I do accept, like anyone else, the reality of the world as it is imposed on me. Otherwise I would end up in the loony bin, singing loony tunes and merry melodies. But at the same time, I know that thought is merely functional in its nature and it cannot help me become something that I am not.

You Invent Your Reality

Q : I have always been told that mankind has a certain purpose in creation. But ever since I read your books, I have begun to wonder whether this is true.

U.G.: You are the one to answer that question. We don't give a tinker's damn, to use that harsh expression, to what others have said about it. How does it matter whether what they have said is true or not? It is up to you to find out. I can say that there is no purpose, and if there is any purpose, we have no way of knowing it. We only repeat what we have been told. We are made to believe that there is a purpose, and that belief is what is responsible for the tragedy of mankind today. We have also been made to believe that we are created for a grander purpose, for a nobler purpose, than all the species in this planet. This is not all. We are also told that the whole creation was created for the benefit of man: that's why we have created all these problems - ecological problems and problems of pollution.

Now, we are almost at a point where we are going to blow ourselves up. The planet is not in danger, but we are in danger. You can pollute this planet and do all kinds of things; the planet can absorb everything - even these human bodies. If we are wiped out, nature knows what to do with the human bodies. It recycles them to maintain the energy level in the universe. That's all it is interested in. So, we are no more purposeful or meaningful than any other thing on this planet. We are not created for any grander purpose than the ants that are there or the flies that are hovering around you or the mosquitoes that are sucking your blood. I can say all this, but what do you have to say? That is more important than what I have to say. We really don't know. We have no way of knowing anything. Even the scientists - they can say what they like. How does it interest us? It does not really matter as to how this whole universe was created - whether God created it, or the whole thing came out of some dust and pebbles, or hydrogen atoms somewhere. It is for the scientists to talk about all this, and every now and then come up with new theories.

They will be amply rewarded and given Nobel prizes. But the theories don't help us to understand anything. So I really don't know if there is any purpose. I don't think that there is any. I do not see any meaning or purpose in life. A living thing, a living organism is not interested in asking the question, "What is the purpose of life? What is the meaning of life?"

Q : Does it matter if you create your own purpose?

U.G.: We are not satisfied with the daily grind of our lives, doing the same thing over and over again. We are bored. So boredom is responsible for asking the question, "What is the purpose?" Man feels that if this is all that is there, what more is there for him to do?

Q : That is how the problem is created.

U.G.: You create a problem and then try to solve it. That's what we are all doing. You enjoy your problems. Why not?

Q : No.

U.G.: Enjoy them.

Q : Enjoy them?

U.G.: But don't go to a therapist. Don't go to a psychiatrist!

Q : Where do we go then?

U.G.: He will take a hundred dollars. I don't know what the charge is here. Probably more in this country. They tell you how to fit into the value system that is created by our culture or society. That is really the human problem. The one very basic question which every intelligent man and woman should ask for himself or herself, "What kind of a human being do I want on this planet?" Unfortunately, the religious thinking of man for centuries has placed before us the model of a perfect being. Nature is not interested in a perfect being. Nature is not interested in the culture input there [in us]. That's the battle that is going on in the form of the demand of the society or culture to fit everybody into its value system. That is really the cause of man's tragedy. It is not a question of destroying the value system or revolting against it. It is the impossibility of fitting yourself into that framework created by your culture that is really the problem. Thought is the real enemy. Thought can only create problems; it cannot solve them.

Q : People are bored...

U.G.: You are bored. Are you not bored?

Q : Yes, I am bored.

U.G.: ... because thought is a repetitive process. It repeats itself over and over again. It is wearing you out.

Q : You said that if we get bored we invent something or other.

U.G.: You create all sorts of things.

Q : But animals do not get bored.

U.G.: No. Not at all.

Q : Why does man get bored?

U.G.: Because man imagines that there is something more interesting, more meaningful, more purposeful to do than what he is actually doing. Anything you want above the basic needs creates this boredom for the human being. But you get the feeling, "Is that all?"

Nature is interested in only two things - to survive and to reproduce one like itself. Anything you superimpose on that, all the cultural input, is responsible for the boredom of man. So we have varieties of religious experiences. You are not satisfied with your own religious teachings or games; so you bring in others from India, Asia or China. They become interesting because they are something new. You pick up a new language and try to speak it and use it to feel more important. But basically, it is the same thing.

Q : Christianity tells us to develop our talents. But you need no talent to reproduce.

U.G.: No talent is required to reproduce. Nature has done a tremendous job in creating this extraordinary piece - the body. The body does not want to learn anything from culture. It doesn't want to know anything from us. We are always interested in telling this body how to function. All our experiences, spiritual or otherwise, are the basic cause of our suffering. The body is not interested in your bliss or your ecstasies. It is not interested in your pleasure. It is not interested in anything that you are interested in. And that is the battle that is going on all the time. But there seems to be no way out.

Q : But if everybody wants to go back to the original state...

U.G.: What is the original state?

Q : I don't know.

U.G.: It's already there. You don't have to do a thing to go back to the original state.

Q : How can you go to that frame of mind? We believe that we have to do something to go back to that state?

U.G.: Your doing something to go back to your original state is what is taking you away from it. The original state is already there and is expressing itself in an extraordinarily intelligent way. The acquired intellect is no match to the intelligence that is there.

Q : Somehow we still do not trust...

U.G.: "Somehow", you say. That is the cultural input.

Q : We have lost touch with the original state some where.

U.G.: ...because culture or society has placed before us the model of a perfect being. Nature does not imitate anything. It does not use anything as a model.

Q : So you can say that all the approaches that mankind has developed to reach the original state are leading man away from it?

U.G.: They haven't worked nor have they touched anything there.

Q : I agree with that. But still can you not give us a model?

U.G.: What is the point in placing before you another model? It will be the same.

Q : Where does it all lead us?

U.G.: It leads you to where you actually stand, and therefore the questions.... [Laughter]

Q : Asking questions about all this is wrong?

U.G.: Don't ask this question. You have no questions, and I have no questions. I have no questions at all other than the basic questions we need to ask. I am here and want to get the bearings of this place. So I want to go and find out. I ask, "Where is this station?" if I want to go to London, I ask, "Where is the British Airways office?" These are the basic questions we need to ask to function sanely and intelligently in this world. We do have to accept the reality of the world as it is imposed on us. Otherwise we will go crazy. If you question the reality of anything that is imposed on you, you are in trouble, because there is no such thing as reality, let alone the ultimate reality. You have no way of experiencing the reality of anything.

Q : Well, we have invented reality...

U.G.: We have invented reality. Otherwise you have no way of experiencing the reality of anything - the reality of that person sitting there, for instance, or even [the reality of] your own physical body. You have no way of experiencing that at all except through the help of the knowledge that has been put in you. So, there may not be any such thing as reality at all, let alone the ultimate reality. I do have to accept the fact that you are a man, that she is a woman. That is all. There it stops. But what is the reality you are talking about?

Q : Of course, she is a woman. We give a reality to it.

U.G.: [Laughter] If you question that, you would be in trouble. You will lose your woman and the woman will lose you. [Laughter] You are not ready for that.

Q : So being born, you have to be taught...

U.G.: Are you sure that you are born? [Laughter] We have been told that.

Q : We have been told that's all. [Laughter] We take it for granted.

U.G.: We take it for granted. You have no way of finding out the fact that you were born on a particular day. What you are not ready to accept is that you are a thing exactly like a computer. You are so mechanical. Everything is put in there. There is nothing that you can call your own. I don't have any thought that I can call my own. What I want to emphasize to those who come to see me is that thoughts are not really spontaneous. They are not self-generated. They always come from outside. Another important thing for us to realize and understand is that the brain is not a creator. It is singularly incapable of creating anything. We have taken for granted that there it is something extraordinary, creating all kinds of things that we are so proud of. It is just a reactor and a container. It plays a very minor role in this living organism.

Q : We are not creating things...

U.G.: You are not creating. The brain is only a computer. Through trial and error you create something. But there are no thoughts there. There is no thinker there. Where are the thoughts? Have you ever tried to find out? What there is, is only *about* thought but not thought. You cannot separate yourself from thought and look at it. What you have there is only a thought *about* that thought, but you do not see the thought itself. You are using those thoughts to achieve certain results, to attain certain things, to become something, to be somebody other than what you actually are. I always give the example of a word-finder. You want to know the meaning of a word and press a button. The word- finder says, “Searching”. It is thinking about it. If there is any information put in there, it comes out with it. That is exactly the way you are thinking. You ask questions and if there are any answers there, they come out. If the answers are not there, the brain says “Sorry”. It is no different from a computer.

Q : You said that you went around just to find out about the surroundings.

U.G.: To learn about my bearings so that I may not get lost here. Even a dog does that. I am no different from a dog. A dog knows its way back home. It knows its master. So I am just like an animal.

Q : When I was a little kid my parents and the people around told me about the bearings of my culture. I was trained not to question them.

U.G.: They don’t want you to question. They force on us everything they believed in, even the things they themselves did not believe, and the things that did not operate in their lives. There is no use blaming them now. We are adults. So we don’t have to blame them. This is a silly idea, the Freudian idea that for everything that is happening your mother is responsible, or your father is responsible. We are all grown-up people. There is no point in blaming our mothers and fathers. Actually, it is not a one-way street. Even children want to be accepted by us. We force them to fit into this framework, and they want to be accepted by us. This is a two-way traffic.

I have said a lot. I repeat the same thing again and again in ten different ways.

Q : Only ten?

U.G.: Or a hundred different ways. [Laughter] I have acquired a rich vocabulary. You can use different words to say the samething.

Q : So, there is no way of seeing what I think I see.

U.G.: You never see anything. The physical eye does not say anything. There is no way you can separate yourself from what you are looking at. We have only the sensory perceptions. They do not tell anything about that thing – for example; that it is a camera. The moment you recognize that it is a camera, and a Sony camera at that, you have separated yourself from it. So what you are actually doing is translating the sensory perceptions within the framework of the knowledge you have of it. We never look at anything. It is too dangerous to look because that 'looking' destroys the continuity of thinking.

We project the knowledge we have of whatever we are looking at. Even if you say that it is an object without giving the name, like, for example, camera, knowledge has already come in. It is good for a philosophy student to talk about this everlastingly, separating the object from the word, or separating the word from the thing. But actually, if you say that it is an object, you have already separated yourself from it. Even if you don't give a name to it, or recognize it as something, or call it a camera, a video camera, you have already separated yourself from it.

All that is already there in the computer. We are not conscious of the fact that we have all that information locked up there in the computer. Suddenly it comes out. We think it is something original. You think that your are looking at it for the first time in your life. You are not. Supposing somebody tells you that this is something new, you are trying to relate what he calls new to the framework of the old knowledge that you have.

Q : So if it is not in the computer, you cannot see it.

U.G.: You cannot see. If the information is not already there, there is no way you can see. [Otherwise] there is only a reflection of the object on the retina. And the scientists who have done a lot of observation and research have given even this statement to us. There is no way of experiencing the fact of that for yourself, because the stimulus and response are one unitary movement. The moment you separate yourself, you have created a problem. You may talk of the unity of life or the oneness of life, and all that kind of stuff and nonsense. But there is no way you can create the unitary movement through any effort of yours. The only way for anyone who is interested in finding out what this is all about is to watch how this separation is occurring, how you are separating yourself from the things that are happening around you and inside of you. Actually there is no difference between the outside and inside. It is thought that creates the frontiers and tells us that this is the inside and something else is outside. If you tell yourself that you are happy, miserable, or bored, you have already separated yourself from that particular sensation that is there inside of you.

Q : So by naming our sensations, our physical processes...

U.G.: The cells are wearing out. That's why I say that the tragedy that is facing mankind is not AIDS or cancer, but Alzheimer's disease. We are using the neurons, our memory, constantly to maintain our identity. Whether you are awake or asleep or dreaming, this process is carried on. But it is wearing you out.

You experience what you know. Without the knowledge you have no way of experiencing anything. There is no such thing as a new experience at all. When you tell yourself that it is a new experience, it is the old that tells you that it is a new experience. Otherwise, you have no way of saying that it is new. It is the old that tells you that it is new. And through that it is making it part of the old.

The only way it [the experience] can maintain its continuity is through the constant demand to know. If you don't know what you are looking at, the 'you' as you know yourself, the 'you' as you experience yourself, is going to come to an end. That is death. That is the only death, and there is no other death.

Q : That's terrifying...

U.G.: That is terrifying - the fear of losing what you know. So actually, you don't want to be free from fear. You do not want the fear to come to an end. All that you are doing - all the therapies and techniques that you are using to free yourself from fear, for whatever reason you want to be free from fear - *is* the thing that is maintaining the fear and giving continuity to it. So you do not want the fear to come to an end. If the fear comes to an end, the fear of what you know comes to an end. You will physically drop dead. A clinical death will take place.

Q : How can you be physically dead if you merely lose some thoughts?

U.G.: When once the 'I' is gone, there is no way of experiencing your own body anymore. You have no way of knowing whether you alive or dead. You will never be able to tell yourself, "This is my body". If you ask me, "Is that your body or my body?" I may say, "This is my body", just to communicate to you, differentiate and say that it is not your body but my body. But the fact that this is my body is something that cannot be experienced at all.

This body is not concerned about what you think, feel, or experience. All feelings are thoughts. There is no way you can feel anything without giving a name to it.

Q : So you say this process of naming is constant.

U.G.: Any movement anywhere - you can't leave that alone. You have to name it.

Q : Because there is identity involved in it.

U.G.: Yes. You can't lose your identity. It's too dangerous. If you don't know what you are looking at, you are going to be in trouble. You may tell yourself that you don't know what you are looking at, but if you are looking at your girl and tell yourself that you do not know [her], that is the end of the whole story. It's too dangerous. Don't play with that kind of thing. You can't sit there and look at the camera and say, "I don't know what I am looking at". But that's a trick. You create a state of mind and believe that you don't know what you are looking at. But actually, in a given situation, if you don't know what you are looking at, there is trouble. So you dare not put yourself in that situation. You can only play games with it.

Q : Is that what is meant by illusion?

U.G.: No. Even if you say it is an illusion you are giving a name to it.

Q : Yes.

U.G.: You see, in India, they call the word illusion, *maya*. *Maya* means 'to measure'. But there is no way you can measure anything unless there is a space, and there is a point [of reference] here. The moment thought takes its birth there, that is the point, and you create another point and try to measure. So thought creates a space. And anything you experience from that point is an illusion. If you say that somebody coming with a gun to shoot you is an illusion, you are a damn fool. You have to protect yourself. It doesn't mean that the whole world is an illusion. Not at all. Whatever you experience of the world, or of yourself, as an entity is an illusion because that experience is born out of the knowledge that is put in there. Otherwise, you have no way of experiencing the reality of anything.

Q : If you have a different background you have a different experience?

U.G.: No. It doesn't really mean it is different. It depends upon what you are interested in. In a computer, for example, a scientist puts in scientific data, a businessman puts in business data, and an artist puts in something else. But the functioning of the computer is the same.

Q : And that determines...

U.G.: The printout is the result of what is put in there. It depends upon your particular interest. You may be a mathematician, a scientist, or a writer.

Q : So if you change the input or material...?

U.G.: No. If you change the material, you replace it with some other material. You get whatever you are interested in.

Q : So, it is a purely physical thing. What can you do to change this?

U.G.: We have not succeeded in changing anything there. You don't realize that all your attempts to bring about change are total failures. What an amount of energy you put into it!

Q : It is not really true because...

U.G.: You feel good because you have given up meat eating.

Q : Yes.

U.G.: Sure, you feel good and enjoy that. What's the difference? Why do you have to feel so good because you have given up meat eating?

Q : It's a physical feeling. I feel better.

U.G.: I don't know - that may be psychological, Sir, if I could use that word. If you want to go back to eating meat, then it is a different story. If there is a craving, it creates a problem. If there is no craving, what's the difference whether you eat meat or vegetables? One form of life lives on another form of life. How many millions of bacteria are crawling all over your body - the flora and the fauna? You will be surprised, if they are magnified. They are as big as cockroaches. [Laughter] They live on you. When it becomes a corpse, they will have a field day on this body.

Q : If it is only physical...

U.G.: What else is there?

Q : I shall eat good food so that they can have a field day.

U.G.: That is your particular fancy. You want to eat macrobiotic food, and someone else wants to eat something else. What's the difference? The body can live on sawdust and glue. You should shoot all these nutritionists on sight and at sight! These commercials sell you all kind of things.

Q : They are making a living out of that.

U.G.: Let them make a living, but we are the sufferers.

Q : They say that if you don't eat food for 14 days you will die.

U.G.: There is no death for this body. After three days there is no way you can feel hunger. What is hunger after all? The level of glucose goes down. After two or three days you don't feel hungry. The body starts living on itself.

Q : When you start having water or food, then changes take place.

U.G.: You need to drink water. Otherwise, after seventy-two hours you are gone. Dehydration takes place. Because eighty percent of the body is water. Not only here, in every plant and in every form of life. Even on this planet, as a whole eighty percent is water.

Q : Why should we feed the body?

U.G.: Yes, why should we feed the body? The body is not

concerned. The body needs some energy, and that energy you can have from anything you eat. Sawdust is enough for it, without the health food and vitamin C, or your brown rice and seaweed.

Q : I think the body will definitely suffer.

U.G.: Not at all. That is your feeling, your idea. It doesn't give a damn. You put ideas in your stomach. First of all you eat ideas... [Laughter]

Q : Most people eat menus...

U.G.: You can eat good ideas. Good luck to you. I am surviving without eating vitamins. I don't eat vegetables. I don't eat fruit. I don't eat brown rice. I have survived seventy-three years. What's wrong with me?

Q : But we are more human...

U.G.: I am also human, more human than most humans are.

Q : I agree. [Laughter]

U.G.: I don't eat ideas. I don't wear names.

Q : If you were a lion and hungry, would you eat meat?

U.G.: If I am that hungry now, I will probably kill you and eat you, like a cannibal! [Laughter] You have been feeding this body with macrobiotic diet. It will do more harm than good. The body knows what is good for it. If it doesn't like some food, it rejects it.

Q : Is alcohol good for the body?

U.G.: Alcoholism is genetically programmed, you know?

Q : There is a belief that certain types of foods are goodfor human beings and certain other types for animals.

U.G.: You can believe whatever you want to believe. Someone else believes something else. It is the belief that matters to people. You replace one belief with another. You are brought up on meat. Then why should you eat macrobiotic diet today? You have changed from one belief to another belief and you feel good. Feel good and enjoy. Enjoy your brown rice.

Q : May I ask another question? Don't you think that we must think positively?

U.G.: Thinking is either positive or negative. As long as you think, it is either positive thinking or negative thinking. When once the positive approach fails, you have invented what is called negative thinking; but the goal is exactly the same.

Q : But you said that although we experience the world as an illusion, it is not an illusion.

U.G.: No. I am not saying that you experience the world as an illusion. What I am saying is that the way you are experiencing things through the help of the knowledge that is put in you is not the way. And you have no way of finding out anything other than that.

Q : But at the same time it is a reality.

U.G.: Look, the body is responding to stimuli. It is a living thing. By calling something 'beautiful', you have already destroyed it. You have put the whole thing in a frame by calling it beautiful. If you don't say it is beautiful, it is having an effect on this body. The body is responding to the stimulus there. You take a deep breath. That's all.

Q : Then why does the same not hold for food?

U.G.: You put in more ideas. You have put ideas into the whole thing. The moment you ask, "How to live" and "What to eat?" you have created a problem.

Q : I believe that there is a certain thing as human food. But there is no culture or religion there.

U.G.: No, no. Everything is cultural. All your tastes are cultivated tastes. The body does not know what you are eating. Even the salt is not salty as far as the body is concerned.

Q : If we had not eaten rice and vegetables, we would not have developed the brains we have developed right now.

U.G.: My brain and your brain are not different. The brain of a genius is no different from yours. They have found out that the brain of Einstein is no different from that of a low-grade moron. [Laughter] It seems that they examined it after his death. They stored it. You will be surprised; it is no different from a walnut. [Laughter] You eat your macrobiotic food and enjoy, Sir. Don't bother about all this.

Q : Oh well, I have enjoyed myself.

U.G.: How long you will enjoy is anyone's guess. Once a

friend of mine invited me and fed me macrobiotic food. I have not yet recovered from that. It was three years ago.

Q : You eat rice then...

U.G.: I don't eat rice even in India.

Q : On the video I saw you eating.

U.G.: I don't think so. If you think so, it's fine with me. The problem is you eat more than what the body needs. It's the over-eating that is the problem.

Q : What about brown rice?

U.G.: Brown rice! The look of it will make me sick! I raised my son on milled rice; double polished and triple polished rice. [Laughs] He is working in a nuclear submarine somewhere in United States. He is an electronics technician. He is healthier than most health food freaks. Now, of course, he eats anything he can get.

Q : You must answer the question...

U.G.: I don't have any answers. You are answering your own questions, I am not answering. Lately I have been using this word, 'ventriloquist'. You know, you ask the question in one voice and answer the question with another voice. All the questions we ask are born out of the answers we already have. Otherwise, you wouldn't have any questions.

Q : If we give up our beliefs, you said that we would die.

U.G.: You replace one belief with another. You can't be

without a belief. What you call 'you' is only a belief. If the belief goes, you go with it. That is the reason why if you are not satisfied with the belief-structure you are brought-up in, you replace it with something else.

Q : Do you believe that there is nothing wrong with the world?

U.G.: I don't see anything wrong with this world, because the world can't be any different. I am not interested in making a living out of telling people that the world needs some change, radical or otherwise. If you are a politician or president of a nation, then it is a different story. Otherwise it is what it is. We being what we are, the world cannot be any different. What I say is not an abstraction. You and I living together is the world.

Q : Last question, Sir. What do you mean when you say I create you?

U.G.: You do create me. I don't create you for the simple reason that I don't have any image of myself. You have an image of yourself and in relationship to that image you create the images of others around you. That is the relationship that you have with the other people. But the people are constantly changing – you are changing and so is the other person. But you want the image always to remain the same. That's just not possible.

Religious Thinking Is Responsible For Man's Tragedy

Q : How did you come to have such a gloomy view of the world?

U.G.: I was surrounded by all kinds of religious people. I felt that there was something funny in their behaviour. There was a wide gap between what they believed and how they lived. This always bothered me. But I could not call all of them hypocrites. I said to myself, "There is something wrong with what they believe. May be their source is wrong. All the teachers of mankind, particularly the spiritual teachers, conned themselves and conned the whole of mankind. So, I have to find for myself, and I have no way of finding out anything for myself as long as I depend upon anyone."

I found that whatever I wanted was what they [the religious

people] wanted me to want. Whatever I thought was whatever they wanted me to think. So there was no way out of that. Somewhere along the line something hit me: "There is nothing there to be transformed, nothing there to be changed. There is no mind there, nor is there any self to realize. What the hell am I doing?" That spark hit me like a shaft of lighting, like an earthquake. It shattered the whole structure of my thought and destroyed everything that was there, all the cultural input. It hit me in a very strange way. Everything that every man had ever thought, felt, and experienced before was drained out of my system. In a way, it totally destroyed my mind, which is nothing but the totality of man's experiences and thoughts. It destroyed even my identity. You see, the identity is nothing but the input of the culture.

Somewhere along the line in human consciousness, there occurred self-consciousness. (When I use the world 'self', I don't mean that there is a self or a center there.) That consciousness separated man from the totality of things. Man, in the beginning was a frightened being. He turned everything that was uncontrollable into something divine or cosmic and worshiped it. It was in that frame of mind that he created "God". So, culture is responsible for whatever you are. I maintain that all the political institutions and ideologies we have today are the outgrowth of the same religious thinking of man. The spiritual teachers are in a way responsible for the tragedy of mankind. We have come to a point where we have to ask a different kind of question and find out if there is anything that we can do.

The way the world is moving, there seems to be no hope. If the world or mankind has to free itself from the chaos of its own making, then man should come up with other ways. As I see it, the whole thing is heading in a direction where there is no way that we can stop or reverse it.

The other day I was talking to someone who asked me, "Why is it that you are not concerned?" I am not interested in saving anyone. As a matter of fact, I have been pleading that the world has to be saved from all the saviours of mankind. Individually there seems to be nothing that you can do to change, alter or reverse anything. And 'collectively' it means war. We have unfortunately placed the politicians in the seats of power. Political consciousness is all that we are left with. But the religious people are still trying to talk in terms of the divine, humanity, ancient culture, *Ramrajya,* this, that, and the other. Politicians also use these things for purposes of elections, and thus try to win people over to there side. But if we think in terms of something that is already dead, we don't have any future to think of. That is why people ask me, "What do you think of Gorbachev?" Gorbachev is a traitor to the cause of communism. Millions of people have died for the cause of communism, and if he is looking to the West for the solutions to his problems, there is something wrong. The answers have to be found within the framework of U.S.S.R.. The West is not in a condition to offer him anything except McDonald's or organically grown potatoes or Pepsi Cola. Actually it is not our ideas of freedom or of humanity that have brought about a change there but it is Pepsi Cola. It has conquered Russia. And it is Coca Cola that has made a tremendous impact on China.

What I am trying to say is that thought has a tremendous control over us. Thought in its birth, in its content, in its expression and in its action is fascist. It wants to control everything. And thought is not an instrument that will help us to solve the problems that we are facing today. W can only ask questions and find out if there are any answers individually. Collectively means, you see, I have one idea, you have another idea, and there is going to be a battle between us.

The identity that we have created, that culture has created in us, is the most important factor, which we have to consider. If we continue to give importance to this identity, which is the product of culture, we are going to end up with Alzheimer's disease. We are putting memory and the brain to a use for which they are not intended. Computers can do the same job in a much more efficient way.

The maintenance of our identity is possible only through the constant use of memory. It is wearing out the human organism, leaving little energy for tackling the problems of the world. You must have read the statistics recently in an American magazine. Alzheimer's disease affects one in three in the sixty-year age group. The nature of this disease is such that it brings about total and complete destruction of the mind and identity. In England one in two in the eighty-year group, altogether six hundred thousand people, are affected, and out of that there are two Nobel Prize winners. Hundreds and thousands of people around the globe are affected. We don't have any record of exactly how many are affected. That may be nature's way of turning us all into vegetables [chuckles] to recreate something better. I am hazarding an opinion that is as bad or as good as anyone else's.

Q : I go along with most of what you say. But there still remains the demolition job, the clearing of cobwebs. We have all these purveyors of religion and godmen...

U.G.: Every time a godman appears on the stage he is adding momentum to all the chaos that already exists, and we are slowly moving in the direction of destroying ourselves.

Q : Yes, I mean that.

U.G.: Not that we all become anti-God, destroying everything. When I talk of a total anarchy, it is a state of being and not a state of doing. There is no action there. Maybe out of that something new will emerge. Now they are talking about new forms of life near a volcano of the west coast of the United States. Maybe something new will spring up. Not that I am concerned about the future of mankind. If humanity goes, you and I will also go with it. Who has given you or me the mandate to save the mankind? I am part of this world. As far as I am concerned I am in perfect harmony with the world. I like it exactly the way it is. I am not in conflict with it. It cannot be any different. You are the guys who want to change the whole thing: "a batter world and a happier world". I don't see any of this possibility you see to create that kind of world. So we must ask questions which have never been asked before, because all the questions which we have been asking are born out of the answers we already have.

But unfortunately, the only way out for all these people is to go back to the great heritage of India. We are the products of the great heritage of the India. But if this what we have done, and if we are what we are today, what is there to be proud of in the great heritage of India? Why do you want us to go back? This great heritage is something that has failed us. What do we do in such a situation? What is the answer? Maybe you have an answer. He has an answer, or she has an answer. I am asking them, since they are the ones that are trying to bring about a change. There is nothing there to be changed. As long as you are interested in bringing about a change in yourself, you talk in terms of bringing about a change in the world. When once you are freed from the demand to bring about any change in yourself, the demand to bring about a change in the world also comes to an end.

All revolutions are nothing but revolutions of our value systems. You only replace one system with another system. But basically, any system is not going to be much different from the system that has been replaced.

Q : Still this hankering 'to know' remains. I reject God; I am an agnostic. Yet, I don't have the answer for the simple question which most of us ask: "Why are we here? What will happen to us when we die?" My only answer is that I have no answer. I don't know. But that does not satisfy us. That is why we turn to people like you.

U.G.: I say, go back to the gurus and they will give you some comfort …

Q : But they spin yarns, which don't make sense to rtional human beings.

U.G.: But they don't want to solve their problems. What I can do?

Q : That's not what I mean. It is a simple question of wanting to know where the beginning was, the purpose and the …

U.G.: Don't you think that wanting to know something is really the problem? Wanting to know is what has created this identity of ours.

Q : Can't we suppress it?

U.G.: No. I am not asking you to suppress it. What I am saying is that 'wanting to know' may not be the answer. Wanting to know more and more is only strengthening and fortifying the very thing, which has not helped us to solve the problem individually or collectively. I am only asking that question. 'Knowing' is not something mysterious or mystical. It simply means to know that this is a chair, or I am happy or unhappy. Look, we have to accept the reality of the world as it is imposed on us. Although it is questionable, this reality is functional in its value. That is the only way we can function sanely and intelligently.

Q : Knowing a concrete object is one thing. But what I have in mind is something like the question posed by Adi Shankara. He asked himself, "Where did I come from?" in a very simple language.

U.G.: That question is irrelevant to me because it does not in any way help us to understand the situation we find ourselves in, as the movement of thought is only interested in establishing a causal relationship.

Q : Would you dismiss the question?

U.G.: I dismiss the question because the question is based on the assumption that there is a cause for everything. To me every event is an independent unit. A friend of mine, Mahesh Bhatt, one of the film directors, signed a contract with Penguin Books to write a biography of his friend U.G. Krishnamurti. I told him that there is no story to tell. I am saying that whatever has happened to me is acausal. Whatever has happened has happened despite everything I did. All those events before it [U.G.'s 'calamity'] were unconnected with it. We would like to link all of them up and create a story or philosophical structure out of them, and say that every event in one's life is not an accident but that some destiny may be shaping the events, shaping one's life. I don't think that is the way we are functioning. This very demand to know either the cause of our own origins or the cause of the origin of the world is an idle demand, the answers for which, however interesting they may be, are of no importance in dealing with the problems of living.

Q : The same problem arises with the question of death: What happens when we die? What does it means to die?

U.G.: We don't want to come to terms with the fact that we can only live seventy or eighty years of life. With death, all that we have achieved during that span has to come to an end. Not wanting to accept the fact that that is the end, we project the beyond and create all kinds of fantasies. My answer to the question is, what do you think is there *now* which will continue after the death of this body? As far as the body is concerned there is neither birth nor death. What we call death is nothing but a reshuffling of atoms, and the reshuffling of atoms takes place for the simple reason that the level of energy in this universe has to be maintained. It is for this very reason, that is, to maintain the level of energy that millions and millions of people have been wiped out through catastrophic events. For nature it is not catastrophic. An earthquake is as much a necessity, as much a part of the planetary activity, as any other event. (Of course, it is no comfort to those who have lost their properties and their near and dear ones. Earthquakes have destroyed large sections of mankind.) So trying to find out answers for those questions is nothing but dialectical thinking. It is not going to help solve the basic problems faced by mankind…

It is needless to answer those questions because there is no end to it. There is no beginning and there is no end. That is not the way things are happening in nature. Everything that is born is destroyed there. You see, birth and death are simultaneous processes. When once the continuity of thought or the demand to experience the same thing over and over again to maintain what we call identity is not there, all these questions that we repeatedly ask are finished. The way thought is taking its birth and then dissolving itself in the form of energy is the way life is. It is not that I have any special insight into nature's laws, but whatever we discover about nature's law is being used for destruction. What little benefit we get is benefiting only a negligible percentage of people on this planet. It is not percolating to the level of the common man. Why are we so tremendously impressed by our scientific research? We can give them Nobel Prizes. We can give them prestigious awards. But how is it [this research] going to affect the common man? Every time somebody comes and knocks on the door of my house, I tell him, "Go to your prime minister. He is there. You elected him. You put him there to feed you, clothe you, and shelter you". You know, if you give charity to a beggar, it's the most vulgar thing. If you do something of that sort, it is only for your self-fulfillment. It is a "do-gooder's" high that you feel. You are not accepting the fact that you are a self-centered man.

We are not doing anything to solve the problems. You would ask me, "What are you doing?" That's a natural question. I am not here working for this country, you see. I am not in any way influenced by the ideas of nationalism, patriotism or any of the stuff that the teachers taught us at school. I never learned anything from either the secular teachers or spiritual teachers. Although I lived with the masterminds, products of Oxford and Cambridge, I didn't benefit by their association.

Q : I ask these questions because as someone with the particular frame work of believing in God and life here after,and as someone who is a journalist, I would like to ask about the injustices in the world.

U.G.: No answers anyone gives are satisfactory answers. The answers in no way explain the existence of poverty and misery. After more than five decades of freedom you still can't go on blaming the British for the situation here [in India]. Don't go on exalting your culture and heritage. In one blast the whole thing should be thrown out. They don't even have the energy to blow up the whole thing. You have been fed with all kinds of bluff and nonsense. For generations you have been under the influence of the belief that there is reincarnation. You believe you did something terrible in your past life, and so you enjoy your misery, your degradation, your poverty in this life and hope for the best in your next life. So what is the point in feeling sorry about all this? For centuries people have been brainwashed to believe in all kinds of things. Besides, you have no way of testing the validity or truth of the statements of those godmen. Someone says he was Shirdi Sai Baba in his previous life and Satya Sai Baba in this life, and his next life he is going to be God knows what. We have no way of testing these claims. You are not going to be there to test that. To those people who ask this question about reincarnation, I tell them that there is reincarnation for those who believe in it, and there is no reincarnation for those who don't believe in it. But if you ask me, "Is there reincarnation [objectively] like the law of gravity in nature?" my answer is, " No". Some people have this compulsion to believe. There is not much that we can do about it. Probably believing [in reincarnation] is consoling and comforting to them.

Q : Well, there is injustice in the scheme of things. When a child is born defective...

U.G.: The explanation that it occurred because of something you did in your past life is a comforting thought. It is a drug that may help you face the situation.

Q : Yet how do I answer such problems?

U.G.: We don't know. We don't have any satisfactory answers. If some chap who claims to be spiritual pretends to have answers to such questions, that gives us comfort.

Q : Well, I dismiss it as bullshit.

U.G.: So do I. But what about the one who believes in such things? It is a comforter for him. You can as well take a drug and forget the whole thing for sometime.

Q : Religion is rightly called the opium of the people.

U.G.: Yes it is. But there is relief from that opium. The body cannot tolerate all these meditation techniques that we impose on it. It [meditation] brings about an imbalance in the chemistry of this living organism. All this is the cultural input there [in us], which is destroying the sensitivity of the whole system. Such actions of yours like breath-control and yoga blur the sensitivity of the sensory perceptions. All this is the enemy of the living organism.

As I was saying, it is the self-consciousness that occurred in the human species somewhere during the course of evolution (I even question evolution; and I don't know if there exists such a thing as evolution at all) that has separated the human species from the totality of nature. It (the self-consciousness) is responsible for the feeling that the human species is created for some grander purpose than all the other species on this planet. It caused the feeling that the whole creation is for the benefit of man. That's how we have created all these ecological problems and problems of every kind. Our trying to take advantage of everything in nature is the source of problems. And, it was at that time what we call 'identity' took its birth. We for some reason seem compelled to maintain that identity.

Q : What part does the brain play in all this?

U.G.: The brain is not a creator. This is a statement, which many people may not accept, but this is what I have found out. Thoughts come from outside. There are no individuals at all. It is culture, society, or whatever you want to call it, which has created all of us for the sole purpose of maintaining its status quo. At the same time, it has also created the idea that you must become something different from what you are. That is why you try to better yourself, improve yourself. You want to become something other than what you are. That creates this neurotic situation.

The neurosis in the human species is absolutely essential. We have to maintain this neurosis in order to function in this society. There is no other way that we can function in this society except to live in hope and die in hope. There are some people who have given up. But we force them to become functional in this value system that we have created. We even push them to commit suicide lest they become manic-depressive individuals. We are solely responsible for driving all these people into a situation where they have put an end to themselves. They don't want to be functional here. They have given up. That is the reason why I say that the psychiatrist is the enemy of this culture, because he is forcing all those people who have given up to fit into this value system. One of the tragic things that human culture has done to us is that it has placed before us the model of a perfect being. That perfect being is modeled after the great spiritual teachers.

Q : Can you elaborate a little more in what you call the value system?

U.G.: The whole value system is born out of the demand to fit ourselves into this model we have before ourselves. We want to develop ourselves into perfect beings. This constant battle within ourselves is created by the value system. We never question that. The value system is false, and it is falsifying us. Nature is trying to create something extraordinary, a perfect species. That is why each individual is unique. Because of this input of culture, it has become impossible for this organism to show uniqueness. We have destroyed the possibility of what nature can do. You only use this paradise that nature has created, including not only mankind but also all the species that exist in this planet. We are solely and fully responsible for the chaos that mankind has created, and there seems to be no way out of it [this chaos]. Every time a so-called saviour comes along he says that he is an *avatar* and that he is the answer to all our problems. This very thing, his claim that he is the answer, adds momentum to the existing chaos. It is making it impossible for us to stop and ask questions which we never asked before. We have got to ask these questions, because all the questions we have been asking are born out of the answers we already have. But no one who suggests we should 'go back' has answers for us at all. And that situation makes it impossible for us to create something new. That is not the way we can resolve our problems. These "go back" and "revive" cries are useless slogans.

Whatever is the great heritage of India, it is good for politicians to use and raise hopes in people's hearts. But we are all the products of that great heritage, and there is nothing to be proud about the people of this country today. We talked of the oneness or unity of life for centuries. Then why is there this poverty? Why is there this misery? Why haven't we done anything to resolve these problems to the satisfaction of everybody? Why even today, after five decades of independence, are we blaming the British for the problems? I can only ask questions. You may very well ask me, "Why don't you do something?" But I am not working for this country, and I have no business to tell the leaders of this country how to run it. We are in a situation where we have to deal only with the political consciousness. Religion is dead, but the religious people are not ready to take back seats and admit to themselves that they have done an enormous mischief and now should leave everything to us. I maintain tha t all the political systems we have today, including communism, are nothing but the warty outgrowth of the religious thinking of man.

Q : What do you think of Gorbachev?

U.G.: You see, Gorbachev is a traitor to the cause of communism. How many thousands of people have died during the Bolshevik revolution! They all have died in vain. What I want to say [to Russia] is that your system has failed, but you have to find answers within that framework and not look to the West to solve your problems. The West is in a sorry mess today. They don't have the answers to their own problems. All those people, the scientists and psychologists who come to see me, I tell them that they have all come to the end of their tether. If they are looking for answers, they should not look to Vedanta, or Zen Buddhism. Those sects don't have any answers for their problems. The scientists and psychologists have to find their answers, if there are any answers within their own framework. Only then will they be able to help mankind to look at things differently. But there is no way you can go back and revive anything.

Q : What should we do?

U.G.: We don't seem to have any answers for our problems. If you ask me about collective answers, there is not much that we can do. And individually there isn't a damn thing that can be done. Not a thing. What it is that we can do? At least, we can ask these questions, the questions that have never been asked, because all the questions that we have been asking for all these years are born out of the answers we already have. But they have not helped us.

Q : There is some grace and shine on your face.

U.G.: Half of me is woman. This is an abnormal thing. This is an abnormal condition of the body that you have turned into some thing mysterious and mystifying and then call it an enlightened being. When once this kind of a thing happens, the whole hormonal balance changes. So, who is normal and who is abnormal? From your point of view this [referring to himself] is an abnormal individual. But I don't call you an abnormal man.

Once a holy man came to see me. He was in his forties. He was claiming that denial of sex is so essential for the spiritual future of man. I said, "It's a crime against nature". Nature has not intended you to deny sex. Then he got up and left. So how can this abnormal situation be made a model for all spiritual aspirants? And why torture them? Why has denial of sex been made the foundation stone of all the spiritual enlightenment in this country and in the West as well? As a reaction or a revolt against that [denial], what you call the Tantric system appeared in this country. When it went out of control, they introduced this mystical element, the "left" and the "right" Tantra. That is why now some people are saying that Tantric sex is one of the means to attain spiritual bliss, enlightenment, and what not.

Q : When you say half of you is female, what do you mean?

U.G.: I said so because whatever has happened to me has changed the whole hormonal balance. It is just not possible for that individual [for U.G.] physically to have sex any more. The whole chemistry of the body has undergone abnormal changes. I call it abnormal because this is not possibly what nature has intended it to be. There are two things that this living organism is interested in - its survival and the reproduction of one like itself. Even nature has discarded this body because it has no use for it any more. But you have turned that into something spiritual. That is why they say that sex control is very essential for the spiritual achievement of human beings. What I am trying to say is that neither the denial nor the indulgence in sex has anything to do with what they call enlightenment.

Q : Do you think that to have sex you need thought?

U.G.: Definitely; otherwise how could it be done? It is just not possible to have a sex "build-up" without thought. It is the continuous thinking that gives the illusion of a coordinator. But here [referring to himself] there is nobody who is coordinating the sensory activity. Sensations occur so fast that there is no way memory can capture that in its framework and say, "This is it". You are looking at some beautiful pet and the next moment when she opens her mouth, probably her teeth would be the ugliest that you have ever seen or can even imagine. You have moved from her beautiful face to her ugly teeth and then on to something else happening somewhere else, and you are looking at that.

I would like to say one thing: to be attracted to something is natural. If you are not attracted, you are a stone. The body with its senses is not a stone. It has to respond to what is happening around it. What touches this body is not your piety or your silence but your anger, your lust, and everything that is happening there.

That is the response I am talking about. Well, I don't translate. I don't even know what is going on here-whether it is a sex drive or affection or anger or greed. None of those things are translated by thought as such and such. There is no time here. That is why I always give the example of a film. If you take a movie of a moving hand, from here to there, there are so many frames. What you see on the screen is an artificial thing. You need a projector to produce that action or movement on the screen. But it is not actually the movement of the hand from here to there. You have to synchronize the discrete movements of the hand to produce a combined effect of the hand moving. That is the way the human organism is operating. When you are listening to the tape-recorded music, you don't hear the gap between the two notes. But the senses register and listen to the gap. This is so even when you speak a language. What is language after all? Language is nothing but the space between the two notes and the tune. If you learn that, you know how to speak Konkani, French or German. In that sense all languages are the same. They are just noise.

Q : Where were you born?

U.G.: I was born in Andhra Pradesh in a place near Vijayawada…

Q : Was your family very conservative?

U.G.: My grandfather, my mother's father, and others in my family were very close to the founders of the Theosophical society. I spent more time in Madras than in Andhra Pradesh. I am better versed in Tamil than in Telugu. I don't know how to read and write Tamil, but Tamil comes to me easier than my mother tongue. I spent all my formative years with the Madras Theosophical Society.

Q : What kind of music do you like?

U.G.: [Laughs] That's very difficult to answer. I can't say that I like or I don't like some music. I don't know. Anything I say, you want to abstract something from it and project something on it. I may have my own likes, but all those likes are conditioned by my upbringing. There is no way you can free yourself from your conditioning. The talk of an unconditioned mind is utterly foolish. But my conditioning does not interfere with my actions. For example, I see somebody. Watching his actions, I would call him 'nasty', or say that he is a nasty man. That is not a value judgement but a descriptive statement of his actions within your framework. But this in no way affects me or changes me in any way that would lead me to react to him the next time. I am not involved with what he is doing. The next moment when somebody else is there, I may say that man is a nice man. But it's the same thing. I really don't mean anything by saying that he is a nice man or that he is a nasty man. I am not involved in any way in his actions.

Q : Sir, what kind of a woman do you like?

U.G.: I don't know. That's the answer.

Q : You don't like women at all?

U.G.: I have no use for them.

Q : Why?

U.G.: As I said a while ago, I like their company. It's a strange question.

Q: Is it not abnormal?

U.G.: That's what I am saying. Whether I hold the hand of a woman or hold the arm of a chair, the physical response is exactly the same. Exactly the same. The response doesn't say that this is the hand of a delicate darling or this is a teak-armed chair. Please don't get me wrong. It is not that I phrase these things in a certain way or that I put them all on the same level. You have to understand what I am trying to say.

Q : But you yourself say that the body has to react to everything in some way?

U.G.: What is going on there, or that reaction you are referring to, is something that I have no way of transmitting or experiencing. I may tell you that I have had sex. Sometimes the memory comes. The moment that memory takes birth there inside of me it is like any other memory. It cannot take root here because every thing here [pointing to his head] tightens and makes it impossible for that [the memory] to drag on or continue any longer. The next moment I will be seeing the black dog there and the frame of the previous thing is finished-the whole thing. I may be now looking at the most beautiful and gorgeous woman, and the next moment it may be a black dog there. These are different frames. That is why I ask, "Who is abnormal here, you or me? Who falls on which side?" My actions are not the actions of an abnormal man. I am not a misogynist. I don't hate women. I like them. I have always had women with me. But the relationship with everything around me is formed and broken every minute of my existence. I don't want you to put me in any particular cage; you will not succeed at all.

Q : Are you married?

U.G.: I was married. I had four children. My wife was one of the most beautiful women around. She was the most beautiful girl in her college also. My daughters are still there [in India]. They are all grown up. Some say that I don't look older than my daughter.

Q : What is the significance of this? Is there any secret?

U.G.: I don't think there is any secret. I don't pay attention to my body. When I was your age, very young, I was stupid. I did all that was expected of those who practice spiritual *sadhana.* But I got nowhere, and I rejected them all. I don't eat any health foods. On the contrary, I say all such things are muck.

I did nothing for my daughters. Had they lived with me what would have happened to them is anybody's guess. They grew-up with my in-laws, you know. And one son is in America. Another died of cancer. He was in an advertising agency in Bombay. He had polio and even went to the U.S. for his treatment. I spent a fortune there, unlike those people who go to America to make money. I wanted to put him back on his feet. I spent many thousands of dollars. He was a very brilliant boy.

Q : How did you get all the money?

U.G.: I was born with a silver spoon in my mouth.

Q : You did not have to work?

U.G.: No. I was born in a rich family. I made a lot of money. The bankers did that for me in Switzerland. That's the reason why I am a non-resident Indian, although I carry an Indian passport. My Swiss money not hidden money. Later I met this Swiss lady.

When everything was gone she came along. She was an extraordinary woman. She lost her memory towards the end of her life. That is the fate of mankind, I am telling you. It is the Alzheimer's disease. If you don't behave, if you continue to maintain your identity, you are in trouble. Nature will destroy the mind and identities of people, and we will all become vegetables. Nature then will reshuffle these human bodies and will create a new species. The human species is expendable. We are not created for any purpose grander than that for which the mosquito that is sucking your blood is created.

Q : Are you a sannyasi?

U.G.: I don't know why you call me a sannyasi. Do I look like a sannyasi?

Q : A modern sannyasi.

U.G.: I am not. I am not a model to anybody. Yesterday some journalists insisted in saying, "If you are a guru or a godman, we can understand. But we cannot figure out what you are. We cannot put you in a cage. That's the problem. We don't know..." Whatever I am can never be fitted into a value system. It has no source or continuity. It cannot help the world to become a better place. The moment you realize exactly what I am trying to say, the 'you' as you know yourself, the 'you' as you experience yourself, will come to an end. Or, you will take whatever I am saying as a threat, because it is undermining the very foundation not only of Indian thinking, but also of human thinking. And then you may even eliminate me.

Q : What you mean is that the Indian heritage has produced only people like our present day politicians.

U.G.: Listen, they don't matter at all. What is happening, whether it is in India or in America or anywhere in the world, is all the same. The players are different but the play is the same. The actors are different but the act is the same. If you pick up a paper published forty years ago in this country, I believe you will be surprised to see that everything they have said is again being repeated by these people now. Exactly the same thing. You don't have to print a new newspaper. You can just pick up that old stuff, and put new names and dates on it and reissue it. What is it that you are doing now? You are doing exactly the same thing.

Q : In India?

U.G.: How can India be a model to the world? You may talk of your spirituality, and go and exploit the people in the United States. But what kind of a model can India give? What kind of effective role can India play in the world? You are doing exactly what they [the Americans] are doing. What is that 'great' culture that you are talking about? How can there be poverty in this country after so many years? I want to know. You talk of the 'oneness of life' or the 'unity of life'. Where is that unity of life? Where is the oneness of life? I want to know. For centuries we have been brainwashed to believe that this is a "*punya bhumi*". I would never accept that designation. Where is that "*punya bhumi*"?

You don't seem to have even social consciousness in you. When you do not have a fellow feeling what is the point of talking of spirituality? There are basic needs. You don't have to devote anything or sacrifice anything to secure them. The poor man has a right to this wealth. That is why I call charity vulgar, vicious. You take everything that belongs to everybody here and then give him charity. What for? He has a right? You may very well ask me the question, "What are *you* doing"? It is easy for you to throw that question at me. I am not here working for this country. If I were in power, I would give everything to everyone. Whatever anyone wants. But you will never put me in the seat of power. They don't want to live in peace. At the same time I will not join a separatist movement and break up this country. I am not interested, because I am not interested in becoming the Chief Minister of Telugu Desam or Kannada Desam or Tamil Nadu. Your system is so corrupt that anyone, however "Mr. Clean" he may be, will also be corrupted. The system is corrupt. You are corrupt. You are corrupted by the religious thinking.

Q : Are you corrupt?

U.G.: No.

Q : Why not?

U.G.: I am not saying that I am incorruptible or anything. I don't touch that [corruption] at all because thought cannot touch any thing here [points to himself] and corrupt it. Your entire heritage is a contamination here [points to himself]. It has been thrown out of my system. All the teachers' teachings are a contamination. But you consider them to be very sacred and keep repeating them, empty words and empty phrases, day after day. The teachings don't operate in your life. You don't have to say anything. If there is a God, let people see what God can make of you. You don't have to talk of God as full of love, mercy, and all that. People will see it in you. So, what good is the culture you are talking about? I want to know. When people throw all these phrases at me, this is what I tell them.

Q : You can afford to talk like this only because you don't have to work.

U.G.: I can work, but then you will not be there. Tomorrow you will be out of your job. You will not be able to compete with me even as a journalist!

Q : Not now.

U.G.: Any time. I reached the top of whatever line I chose. When I was twenty-one I was the leader of the Theosophical Society. I made a million dollars out of a hundred thousand dollars. I chose this life not because I was a total failure or misfit. I chose this life because I wanted to find the source [of why people behave the way they do]. "Why is there this dichotomy in people? They talk of one thing and their behaviour patterns are something else. Something is funny". I did not condemn people as hypocrites. I said, "Maybe the source is wrong. The man who is responsible for the teaching is wrong. Maybe he conned himself and conned everyone else". So I wanted to find out.

Now, I know that they all conned themselves and conned the whole mankind. I conned myself too. I believed in them. I placed my confidence in them but they led me nowhere. Having known this, I cannot do to others what they did to the whole of mankind. I can just point out "Look here! They have put us all on the wrong track. If you want to find out for yourself and by yourself, go ahead and do it". I am not here to liberate anybody. I am telling my friend here, "Go to hell! Stay there and rot in it. I will not lift my little finger to help you because you enjoy your hell. You love it". Who am I to liberate you? When once the demand to bring about a change in you is not there, the demand to change the world is not there. What is wrong with this world? It cannot be any different. I am not in conflict with this world. You may offer me a utopia tomorrow, and a *Ramrajya* the day after tomorrow. But this is the *Ramrajya* they have promised us. You can look at it right now. I am only pointing out all this when these people throw high-sounding phrases at me.

Q : But there is no peace throughout the world?

U.G.: How can you create peace through war? What is the source of war? This peace is war. You are promising peace of mind through meditation, which is war. I discovered these things when I was very young. Can you establish peace through war? The peace that is there between world wars is false. You are war-weary and getting ready for another war. I am not saying anything against war. I am not a peace-monger, much less a war-monger.

Seeking Strengthens Separation

Q : What do you mean by saying, "You are the medium through which I can express myself"?

U.G.: Yes. You are the medium through which I can express myself. There is no other way. I don't even have the impetus to express myself. You may very well ask me, "Why the hell do you talk? Why the hell do you meet people?" It is you who have brought all these people. [Laughter] Why do you ask me questions? That is one of the reasons why I have always avoided publicity of any kind. I don't want to promote myself, nor am I allowing others to promote me.

Q : You have no need to express yourself at all?

U.G.: No, not at all. Not even the impetus to talk. I don't have it.

Q : Then you are very talented...

U.G.: I am not. He comes or she comes or you come. I am like a puppet sitting here. It's not just I; all of us are puppets. Nature is pulling the strings, but we believe that we are acting. If you function that way [as puppets], then the problems are simple. But we have superimposed on that [the idea of] a 'person' who is pulling those strings.

Q : What is nature?

U.G.: All of us are the same. That's what I am saying.

Q : If you are saying that someone is pulling the strings and that we are mere puppets, what is the life force that is called nature?

U.G.: I understand your problem. The actions of life are outside the field of thought. Life is simply a process of stimulus and response; and stimulus and response are one unitary movement. But it is thought that separates them and says that this is the response and that is the stimulus. Any action that is born out of thinking is destructive in its nature because thought is a self-perpetuating mechanism. Any action that is outside the field of thought is one continues movement. It is one with the movement of life. It is that flow of things that I am referring to, you see. You don't even have to paddle out of the mainstream on to the banks there. But you are frightened of sinking in it.

Q : We are not frightened.

U.G.: "We are not..." [Laughter] What are you saying? Are you sure?

Q : There is still a side stepping of nature. What is that?

U.G.: Yes. That's it. That is exactly what I am saying. To side step the complexities of this society is one of the biggest mistakes that we are making. But there is nothing out there, you see. All these godmen, gurus, and the flunkies (the most wicked word to use) are offering us a new oasis. You will find out that it is no different from other mirages. We are leaving everything for some mythical certainty offered to us. But this is the only reality and there is no other reality.

What I am emphasizing is, if your energy is not wasted in pursuit of some mythical certainties offered to us, life becomes very simple. But we end up being wasted, misled and misspent individuals. If that energy is released, what is it that we can't do to survive in the midst of these complexities of the world created by our culture? It is very simple. The attempt to sidestep these complexities is the very thing that is causing us all these problems.

Q : What is energy? What is nature?

U.G.: Energy is something which cannot be defined and which cannot be understood. Not that I am mystifying it. The moment the dead thought tries to capture that energy, it [thought] is destroyed. Thought is matter. The moment it is created, it has to be destroyed. But that is the very thing that we resist, you see. Thought is born and is destroyed, and again it is born and again it is destroyed. The only way you can give continuity to thought is through this constant demand to experience everything. This is the only way you try to maintain the continuity of the 'experiencing structure'.

One thing that I emphasize all the time is that without knowledge you can't experience anything. What you do not know, you cannot experience. It is the knowledge that creates the experience, and it is the experience that strengthens the knowledge. At every moment of our existence, we have to know what is happening outside of us and what is happening inside of us. That is the only way you can maintain this continuity.

Q : I get the impression that what you are proposing is in a way a revolutionary idea. When you say, "All these godmen", it's a kind of revolt.

U.G.: They are giving you false comfort, and that is what people want. What I am saying is what the mainstream of population is interested in, either here or anywhere in the world. They hear what they want to hear. What I say is of no interest to them. If you say that God is redundant, it is not a rebellion against anything: you know religious thinking is outdated and outmoded. But I go one step further and say that all political ideologies are nothing but the warty outgrowth of the same religious thinking of man. They may call it a revolution. But revolution is only a revolution of things. You will only end up creating another value system, which may be slightly different from the value system that we want to destroy. But basically they are all the same. That is why when it [the revolution] settles down, it calls for another revolution. Even the talk of continuous revolution of Mao-Tse-Tung has failed. In the very nature of things, a revolution has to settle down.

Q : Well, each one has his path. The Buddha, Jesus, and other teachers had what they thought was the path towards that consciousness.

U.G.: I am questioning the very idea of consciousness. There is no such thing as consciousness at all. Consciousness is nothing but knowledge. Don't ask me how knowledge originated. Somewhere along the line knowledge started with you, and then you wanted to know about the things around. That is what I mean by "self-consciousness". You have become conscious of what is going on around you, and so naturally you want to know. What I am suggesting is that the very demand to understand the mystery of existence is destructive. Just leave the mystery alone.

Q : You can say that after searching for a long time, right?

U.G.: What I am saying is not born out of my keen observation of things around me. It is not born out of logical thinking. It is not a logically ascertained premise.

Q: What was your makeup?

U.G.: There was this makeup within me from the very beginning of rejecting everything totally. I lived amongst masterminds. They were not ordinary people. I have travelled everywhere, and, as I very often say, I was not born yesterday.

What I am saying is that this is something that you cannot totally reject through any volition or effort of yours. Somehow it happened to me. It is just a happening. It is acausal. The whole thing drained out of my system - the parameters that mankind has evolved, the thoughts, feelings and experiences throughout the ages. All this was thrown out of my system.

Q : But why doesn't it happen to me?

U.G.: The potential, the possibility is there, but the probability is zero. It is because you are all the time trying, and that is not letting what is there to express itself. Thought creates an armour all around itself. Any time a crack appears there, you patch it up…

Q : Coming back to what you said earlier about rejecting the whole past – the experiences, thoughts and everything…

U.G.: It is not something that you can do through any effort, will or volition of yours. It's a miracle. So what I am emphasizing is that whatever has happened to me has happened despite everything I did. In fact, everything I did only blocked it. It prevented the possibility of whatever was there to express itself. Not that I have gained anything. Only what is there is able to express itself without any hindrance, without any constraints or restraints imposed on it by society for its own reasons, for its own continuity and stability.

Q : Shouldn't we have to search first?

U.G.: The search is inevitable and is an integral part of it. That is why it has turned us all into neurotics and has created this duality for us. You see, ambition is a reality; competition is a reality. But you have superimposed on that reality the idea that you should not be ambitious. It has turned us all into neurotic individuals. We want two things at the same time.

Whether he is here or in America or in Russia or anywhere else, what does man want? He wants happiness without one moment of unhappiness. He wants permanent pleasure without pain. This is the basic demand - permanence. So it is this demand that has created the whole religious thinking - God, Truth or Reality. Since things in life are not permanent, we demand that there must be something permanent. That is why these religious teachers are peddling their wares in the streets. They offer you these comforts: 'permanent happiness' or 'permanent bliss'. Are they ready to accept the fact that bliss, beatitude, immensity, love and compassion are also sensual?

Q: You mean there is nothing to what Christ or Buddha said.

U.G.: Let's leave them alone. Otherwise we will all be in trouble.

Q: Well I want to know...

U.G.: They are all false as far as I am concerned. This certainty that I have, is something that I cannot transmit to you. It does not mean that I will go and burn all the churches, temples, or bury all the Vedas etc, or that I will become a terrorist and mindlessly killed everyone. That's all too silly. It's neither 'Love thy neighbour as thyself', nor the spiritual values, nor the human value system that can protect us from now on, but the terror that your very existence is at stake. You cannot survive unless the one that is next to you also survives. It's not cooperation on the basis of love and brotherhood, but it's the way this human body is functioning, the way that animals are functioning that can protect you. Animals do not kill their fellow beings (they are also beings, you see) for an ideology or for God.

You are not decent and decorous enough to admit that all your spiritual experiences - bliss, be atitude or love -are also sensual activities. Any activity of thought, whether it is called spiritual or sensual, is also a sensual activity. That's all that you are interested in. Your being in a blissful mood is a high, the do-gooder's high. You become a boy scout and take the lady across the road so that you can get some brownies. This is the do-gooder's high that they talk about. Jogging also gives you a high. Let's admit it.

Q : But is that high necessary for someone?

U.G.: It is necessary for the survival of the experiencing structure, and not for this body. The body is rejecting all that. It doesn't want any of those things.

Q : The experiencing structure is separate?

U.G.: Yes, that is separate and outside of us. You are trying to make everything part of the thought-sphere.

Q : You say that there is no individual.

U.G.: Where is the individual?

Q : Well, I feel I am one.

U.G.: You are not an individual. You are doing exactly the same thing that everybody is doing.

Q : But still I feel that I am an individual.

U.G.: Your feeling it does not mean anything. The individual you are talking about is created by your culture. You are creating that non-existing individual there.

Q : Am I not separate from this body and that body?

U.G.: No, not at all.

Q : How are we connected?

U.G.: If you accept what I am talking about, it is a very dangerous situation. Your wife goes, you see.

Q : No relationship…?

U.G.: No relationship. Sorry…

Q : I don't want it.

U.G.: You don't want it? "How can you ask for this?" is all that I am saying. You are only trying to fit me into a framework by calling me an enlightened man. This fellow [U.G. points to his guest in Delhi] is telling everyone, "Jesus is living here. Why should I go to the Church?" He is crazy. [Laughter] Don't you think that they [the religious people] have all created a mess for us? They laid the foundation for the destruction.

Q : Well, you are destroying them…

U.G.: I am not destroying anything.

Q : Let me just complete my part.

U.G.: All right.

Q : The Buddha said, "Go through this kind of thing." So did Jesus, to reach whatever – enlightenment or Moksha…

U.G.: But you have not arrived anywhere. Even the claimants have not arrived anywhere.

Q : From what I understood, you don't have to reach for answers, because all the answers are really coming from the answers that you already have.

U.G.: But is there any way you can free yourself from that activity?

Q : Isn't it in a way a part or expression of that state?

U.G.: There is no other way I can point out the danger that is involved in your seeking whatever you are seeking. You see, there is this pleasure movement. I am not against the pleasure movement. I am neither preaching hedonism nor advocating any '-ism' or anything. What I am saying is a threat to 'you as you know yourself and experience yourself. You necessarily have to fit me into that framework [of the Buddha, Jesus, and others], and if don't succeed, you will say, "How can he be outside of it?" The way out for you is either to reject me totally, or to call me a fraud or a fake. You see, the feeling, "How can all of them be wrong?" prevents you from listening to me. Or else you put it another way and say that the content of whatever has happened to U.G. and to them is the same, but his expression is different.

Q : Taking this a little further, I feel whatever is right to you in terms of an awareness level need not be right to me. You may not be interested in me...

U.G.: I am not concerned about you at all. You can stay in hell, rot in hell, and do what you like. I am not here to save you. I don't mean you personally.

Q : Yes, I understand.

U.G.: What I am saying has no social content. I have opinions on everything in this world. You have your opinions, and I can also express opinions and judgements on everything. But my opinions and judgements are no more important than the opinions and judgements of your mother or that taxi driver there. Because you are an I.A.S. officer, do you think that your opinions are more valid? I was lecturing on the essential unity of all religions everywhere around the globe. [Laughter]

Q : But what you have discovered...

U.G.: I haven't discovered anything. That's what's strange.

Q : What was it you wanted, Sir?

U.G.: I wanted *moksha*, what the Buddha had. Just the way you think about what I have or what Jesus Christ had.

Q : You mean a continuous state of happiness. [Laugh-ter]

U.G.: You see, the Buddha created U.G.; Jesus created Frank. You don't understand that, do you? You don't want this [U.G.] to go [out of your system], and that is the reason why you keep that [the Buddha, Christ, etc.] and perpetuate it. Both are the same. Culture has created the individual for the sole purpose of maintaining its continuity. Every time you condemn anger, that strengthens and fortifies the movement of your culture and your value system. Every time you praise the Lord, you are maintaining and perpetuating that self. Culture has created you and me for the sole purpose of maintaining its status quo. You don't want a change. You have invented something that is there today, and it will continue to be there after you are gone.

Q : Why do they pass on that misery to us?

U.G.: Why are you passing on this misery to your little girl there?

Q : You have spoken of some *chakras* in your book, Sir.

U.G.: Well, some people were asking me some questions and I happened to answer them. That is why I call it a mistake. [Laughter] [Reference to U.G.'s book entitled Mystique of Enlightenment.] Many people want to fit me into traditional descriptions of things like Yoga.

What happens is that the servant has taken possession of the running of the house in trying to influence everything there. Somehow, through some miracle he is forced to leave. When the servant leaves, he wants to adopt a scorched-earth policy. He wants to burn everything there. You want him to go but he won't go. He has become the master. So this [your thought] is moving at a particular rhythm, at a particular tempo and speed. Suddenly when it stops, through no volition of your, through no effort of yours, it blows up the whole thing here. That's all that has happened to me. From then on it [the organism] falls into a quite natural rhythm and functions in its own way. That is why all those changes take place in the body.

Q : You mean the servants inside have taken over this body?

U.G.: The servant is outside controlling you.

Q : So, then, where is the blowing up?

U.G.: No blowing up. Nothing is there.

Q : But what is the natural state that you are talking about?

U.G.: The natural state is the functioning of this living organism. It is not a synonymous term for enlightenment or God-realization or self-realization. What is the left here is this pulsating living organism. And the way it is functioning is no different from the mosquito that is sucking your blood.

Q : That itself may be called awareness.

U.G.: Not awareness. I don't like to use that word. It is not something that can be captured, contained and given expression to through your experiencing structure. It is outside the field of experience. So it cannot be shared with anyone. That's the reason why I am saying that he, you, or it, is the medium through which whatever I am saying is expressing itself. But you are distorting, correlating and garbling it. Thought cannot help doing that.

Q : Trying to determine whether you are showing us a path or whether this path is right or wrong...

U.G.: No, when there is no path, where is the question of right or wrong?

Q : Maybe, you can't give me the path.

U.G.: No. If he is making a path out of what I am saying, it is his tragedy. If he takes another path, it is his misery.

Q : Let us talk of the big bang theory of the universe.

U.G.: I question the big bang theory.

Q : But you know that we were all atoms in the begining

U.G.: I am questioning even the fundamental particles. We will never be able to find the fundamental particles.

Q : In your first book you talk of the ionization of thought and an explosion.

U.G.: From then on, understanding is not through the instrument which we are using all the time to understand - the intellect. We have developed and sharpened the intellect through years. So it [the intellect, in U.G.] understood in its own way that it is not the instrument, that there is no other instrument, and that there is nothing to understand. My problem was how to use this intellect to understand whatever I was looking for. But it didn't help me to understand a thing. So I was searching for some other instrument to understand, that is, intuition, this, that, and the other. But I realized that this is the only instrument I have; and the hope that I would understand something through some other instrument, on some other level, and some other way, disappeared. It dawned on me, "There is nothing to understand". When this happened, it hit me like a shaft of lightning. From then on, the very demand to understand anything was finished. That understanding is the one that is expressing itself now. And it cannot be used as an instrument to guide, direct or help me, you or anybody.

Q : Don't you think that it happened only because...

U.G.: That explosion that occurred is happening all the time. It is all the time exploding. Any attempt on my part to understand anything at any given moment is exploded because that [thought] is the only instrument I have, and there is no other instrument. This instrument cannot invent a thing called hope again anymore. There is no hope of understanding. The moment it [thought] is forming something there, it is exploded, not through any volition, not through any effort, but that's exactly the way it happens. It is continuously happening all the time. That is the way life is moving along, it has no direction.

The body has no need to understand anything. The body does not have to learn anything, because anything you learn, anything you do is attempting to change, alter, shape or mould yourself into something better. This [body] is a perfect piece that has been created by nature. In this assemblage of the species of human beings on this planet, one being is endowed with the intelligence of an Einstein, another is endowed with the brawn of a Tyson and someone else is endowed with the beauty of a Marilyn Monroe. But two or three or all [of these characteristics] in one will be a great tragedy. I can't conceive any possibility of all the three blooming in one individual – brain, brawn, and beauty.

Q : Are you afraid of death?

U.G.: There is nothing to die here [in U.G.]. The body cannot be afraid of death. The movement that is created by society or culture is what does not want to come to an end. How it came to an end [in U.G.] I really don't know. What you are afraid of is not death. In fact, you don't want to be free from fear.

Q : Why?

U.G.: Because when the fear comes to an end you will drop dead.

Q : Why?

U.G.: That is its nature. It is the fear that makes you believe that you are living and that you will be dead. What we do not want is the fear to come to an end. That is why we have invented all these new minds, new science, new talk, therapies, choice less awareness and various other gimmicks. Fear is the very thing that you do not want to be free from, what you call 'yourself' *is* fear. The 'you' is born out of fear; it lives in fear, functions in fear and dies in fear.

Q : The body is not interested in dying...

U.G.: When the body encounters a cobra it steps back, and then you take a walk. The cobra is a marvelous creature. If you hurt it you are hurting yourself. I mean it [hurting it] physically hurts you [back], not psychologically or romantically – because it is all one movement of life. What I am saying is that you will never hurt that. The cooperation there springs from the total selfishness of mutual survival. It's like the cell in your body, which also can survive only when it cooperates with the cell next to it. Otherwise it has no chance of survival. That's the only way we can live together. But that has to percolate to the level of, if you want to use that word, your 'consciousness'. Only then you will live in this world peacefully.

Q : Well, is it [all life] totally interdependent?

U.G.: It is that total interdependence for survival on the physical level that can bring about unity. Only on that level.

Q : The body and the intellect are separate.

U.G.: The intellect is created by culture and is acquired. The intelligence that is necessary for survival is already there in the physical organism. You don't have to learn a thing. You need to be taught, you need to learn things only to survive in this world that we have created, the world of ideas. You need to *know* in order to survive. You have to fight for your share in the cake. Somebody comes along and says that you should fight without expecting any results. What the hell are you talking about? How can you act without expecting any results? As long as you live in this world you have to fight for your share. That is why they teach you, send you to school, and give you some tools. That is what society has done to you. But religion comes along and tells you that you should fight for your share without expecting anything in return. That is why you are turned into a neurotic individual. Otherwise you will fight only for your share. You don't grab the whole thing. You grab the whole thing because you have been taught by religion, culture or something else to do so. Animals kill only for their survival and leave the rest of their game. You can call it garbage or whatever you want. Every other thing survives on that. If I take only whatever I need for myself, the rest is there for everybody. There won't be any shortage.

Q : Were you with the Theosophical Society and J. Krishnamurti?

U.G.: I left the society in 1953, and my contact with the Theosophical Society and Krishnamurti ended in 1956. I almost grew up there. I lived in Madras for 21 years, ever since I was fourteen. I was very actively associated with the Theosophical Society as the Joint Secretary of the Indian section; I was first a national lecturer and then an international lecturer. It's all ancient History now.

Q : It is difficult to put you in a definite category.

U.G.: All those who come to see me have this problem of where to fit me. It is easy for them to call me godman, enlightened man, guru and stick all these fancy labels on me. "That is our difficulty", they say. "We really don't know where to fit you. It is a reflection on our intelligence", they say. Even philosophers talk of the impossibility of fitting me into a framework. Not that I am feeling superior or proud.

Q : But where will you fit yourself?

U.G.: I don't know. I won't say I am a misfit. I am part of the mainstream of life everywhere. At the same time I have no roots anywhere. If I may put it that way, I am a rootless man of sorts. I have lived everywhere in this world, and I don't feel at home any where. It's very strange. I am one of the most traveled persons in this world. I have been travelling ever since I was fourteen, and since then I never lived in any place for more than six months at a time. My travelling is not born out of my compulsive need to travel. When people ask me, "Why do you travel?" I answer them, "Why do some birds travel from Siberia to a small bird sanctuary in Mysore State and then go back all the way?" I am like those migratory birds. It's very strange. I have travelled everywhere except in China. I have gone to all the communist countries. And in America I have spent several years. Nowadays I divide my time between Bangalore, Switzerland and the U.S.

Q : If the world can't find a label for you, what kind of a label do you find for the world?

U.G.: I am quite satisfied with the world! [Laughter] Quite satisfied. The world cannot be any different. Travelling destroys many illusions and creates new illusions for us. I have discovered, to my dismay, if I may put it that way, that human nature is exactly the same whether a person is a Russian, or an American or someone from somewhere else. It is as though we all speak the same language, but the accent is different. I will probably speak [English] with an Andhra accent, you with a Kannada accent, and someone else with a French accent. But basically human beings are exactly the same. There is absolutely no difference. I don't see any difference at all. Culture is probably responsible for the differences. We being what we are, the world cannot be any different. As long as there is a demand in you to bring about a change in yourself, you want to bring about a change in the world. Because you can't fit into the framework of culture and its value system, you want to change the world so that you can have a comfortable place in the world.

Q : You say that you are satisfied with the world. Why do you say that?

U.G.: What makes you think that the world can be any different? Why do you want to change the world? All these utopias, all these ideas of creating a heaven on this earth are born out of the assumption that there is a heaven somewhere there and that we have to create that heaven on this planet. And that's the reason why we have turned this into a hell. You see, I don't call this a hell. I'd like to say it can not be any different.

Nature has provided us with tremendous wealth on this

planet. If what they say is correct, twelve billion people can be fed with the resources that we already have on this planet. If eighty percent of the people are underfed, then there is something wrong - something is wrong because we have cornered at one place all the resources of this world. I don't know. I am not competent enough to say, but they say that the Americans alone consume eighty percent of this world's resources. What is it that is responsible for that?

The problem is this: nature has assembled all these species on this planet. The human species is no more important than any other species on this planet. For some reason, man accorded himself a superior place in this scheme of things. He thinks that he is created for some grander purpose than, if I could give a crude example, the mosquito that is sucking his blood. What is responsible for this is the value system that we have created. And the value system has come out of the religious thinking of man. Man has created religion because it gives him a cover. This demand to fulfill himself, to seek something out there was made imperative because of this self-consciousness in you which occurred somewhere along the line of the evolutionary process. Man separated himself from the totality of nature. The religious thinking of man originated from the idols, gods, and spiritual teachers that we have created. So the whole trend is in the direction of creating a perfect man, whereas...

Q : Without this we feel a kind of insecurity. We need something.

U.G.: That is why we have invented all this. You might as well take Valium, or use something, and forget about it. That [security] is all that you are interested in. And I don't want to run down the gurus and the godmen we are flooding the world with.

Q : Even if we do seek, I feel that is also a part of nature.

U.G.: If that is so, then why are you trying to change it? Why don't you accept it? You see, the problem is the demand to bring about a change.

Q : What is it that distinguishes us from animals? We think we are different, right?

U.G.: Thinking is responsible, and thinking is born out of this self-consciousness. When I use the word self-consciousness I don't mean all that stuff we find in religious thinking. What I mean is very simple: I mean the feeling that you are different from the tape recorder there, that you are different from that blue door. This is what I mean by separation. That feeling doesn't exist in animals at all. We are made to believe that there is something that you can do, to bring about a change in and around you. The demand for change springs from this self-consciousness, the separation from the singleness of the whole nature around us.

Q : Without that separation...

U.G.: Don't say, "Without separation"!

Q : Wait a minute, without separating myself from the things around, I feel that I am unable to act.

U.G.: Yes, that's why I say that any action that is born out of your thinking, or let's say thought, is destructive. It is destroying the peace that is there. The way this living organism is functioning is marvellous. The human organism is a perfect specimen of the creation of the nature. Nature is only interested in perfecting the species. But we have superimposed on that the idea of a perfect man, and that idea is the problem. This idea is born out of the assumption that there is perfect man like all these Buddhas, Jesuses, and others. You are trying to model you life after these great teachers. You want your behaviour patterns to be like theirs. But it's just not possible. A 'perfect being' does not exist at all. A perfect being is the end product of human culture, that is, the being we think as the perfect being. And you want everybody to be perfect that way. So going back to my point, nature's interest is only to create perfect species. It does not use any model. Every human being is something extraordinary and unique. If a being does not fit into the scheme of things, nature discards it and starts all over again.

Q: But if you look at the animal family, there is a desire in them to change the environment in a set frame. They want to eat more.

U.G.: They don't eat for pleasure. They eat for survival. Actually, whatever you project on animals is born out of your own ideation and mentations. It is born out of your subjectivist approach to the problem, which is also born out of your value system. We want to understand animals or the laws of nature with the idea of "What do I get out of that?". Our desire to know the laws of nature is only to use them for perpetuating something here [in the human being]. So thought is, in its birth, in its content, in its expression, and also in its action, to use a very crude political word, fascist in nature. [Laughs] There is no way you can get away from that. It [thought] is a self-perpetuating mechanism.

Q: What I can make out of what you are saying is that we are operating under a value system, whether it is good or bad. But have you skipped that somewhere?

U.G.: I have not skipped that. You see, both good and bad, right and wrong, are not the reverse of a coin but are the same coin. They are like the two ends of the spectrum. One cannot exist independent of the other. When once you are finished with this duality, (I am using the word with much caution, although I don't like to use it) when you are no longer caught up in the dichotomy of right and wrong or good and bad, you can never do anything wrong. As long as you are caught up in it, the danger is that you will always do wrong; and if you don't do wrong, it is because you are a frightened 'chicken'. It is out of this cowardice that the whole religious thinking is born.

Q : You were saying in some context that anger is not bad, and that anger cannot do any harm.

U.G.: Anger is like an outburst of energy. It is like the high tide and the low tide in the sea. The problem is, "What to do with anger?" The question, "What to do with anger?" is something put in there by culture, because society considers an angry man a threat to its status quo, to its continuity.

Q : Does it?

U.G.: Yes, of course.

Q : Well, you are not a threat then.

U.G.: I am not a threat. I am not a threat because I cannot, you see, conceive of the possibility of anything other than this. I am not interested in changing anything. You are the one that is all the time talking of bringing about a change. At the same time everything around you and inside of you is in a flux. It is constantly changing. Everything around you is changing; yet you don't want change. You see, that's the problem. Your unwillingness to change is really the problem, and you call it a tradition.

Q : That can happen only if what has happened to you happens to us...

U.G.: Nothing *has* happened to me.

Q : You function bodily.

U.G.: You and I are functioning in exactly the same way; and I am not anything that you are not. You think I am different from you. You have to take my word: at no time does the thought that I am different from you ever enter my mind. I know for certain that you are functioning in exactly the same way that I am functioning. But you are trying to channel the activity or movement of life both to get something and to maintain that continuity of what is put in there [in you] by culture. That is not the case here [in U.G.].

We think that thoughts are there inside of us. We think that they are self-generated and spontaneous. What is exactly there is what I call a thought-sphere. The thought-sphere is the totality of man's experiences, thoughts, and feelings passed on to us from generation to generation. In this context I want to mention that the brain is not a creator, but only a reactor. It is only reacting to stimuli. What you call thought is only the activity of the neurons in the brain. In other words, thought is memory. A stimulus activates the brain through the sensory perceptions and then brings memory into operation. It is nothing marvellous. It is just a computer with a lot of garbage put in there. So it is not a creator. The brain is not interested in solving any of the problems created by us. It is singularly incapable of dealing with the problems created by thought. Thought is outside and it is extraneous to the brain.

Q: What you are saying gives us the impression that nothing is to be changed. But there is this fear that then the brain will becom e very inactive, die away, or some such thing.

U.G.: No, no.

Q : But if we can go back a little into this, thought is necessary in some way. I don't know how instincts developed first and where thought picks up...

U.G.: It is a very superficial division that we make between thought and instinct. Actually there are no instincts in the human being at all. There is no such thing as instinct. That's all invented by your fanciful thinking.

Q : All right, we take it then that the thought process is outside of us.

U.G.: Thought processes then and even now are outside of you. Self-consciousness or separation [of ourselves] from the world around us occurs, they say, - I am not competent enough to say anything – around the eighteenth month of the child. Until then the child cannot separate itself from whatever is happening there inside and outside of itself. But actually there is no inside and outside at all. What creates the inside and outside, or what creates the division between the inside and the outside is the movement of thought. Anything that is born out of thought is a self-protecting mechanism.

Q : Why do you think that we have that?

U.G.: You want an answer for that? The answer for that is that nature uses the human species to destroy everything that it has created. Everything that is born out of thought, every discovery you have made so far is used for destructive purposes. Every invention of ours, every discovery of ours is pushing us in that direction of total annihilation of the human species.

Q : But why? Why does nature deliberately want to first create and then destroy?

U.G.: Because really nothing is ever born, and nothing ever dies. What has created the space between creation and destruction, or the time between the two, is thought. In nature there is no death or destruction at all. What occurs is the reshuffling of atoms. If there is a need or necessity to maintain the balance of energy in this universe, death occurs. You may not like it. We may condemn earthquakes. Surely they cause misery to so many thousands of people. And all this humanitarian activity around the world to send planeloads of supplies is really a commendable act. It helps those who are suffering there and those who have lost their properties. But it is the same kind of activity that is responsible for killing millions of people. What I am saying is that the destructive, war-making movement and the humanitarian movement on the other hand - both of them are born from the same source.

In the long run, earthquakes and the eruption of volcanoes are part of nature's way of creating something new. Now, you know, something strange is happening in America – the volcanic eruptions. Some unknown forms of life are growing there in that very thing which was destroyed. Of course, I am not saying that you should not do anything in the way of helping those people.

The self-consciousness that occurred in the human species

may be a necessary thing. I don't know. I am not claiming that I have a special insight into the workings of natrre. Your question can be answered only that way. You see for yourself. That's why I say that the very foundation of the human culture is to kill and to be killed. It has happened so. If one is interested in looking at history right from the beginning, the whole foundation of humanity is built on the idea that those who are not with us are against us. That's what is operating in human thinking. So, to kill and to be killed in the name of God, represented by the church in the West, and all the other religious thinking here in the East, was the order of the day. That's why there is this fundamentalism here in this country now. The Chinese - what horrors they are committed, you will be surprised: they killed scholars and religious people. They burned and buried the books of Confucius and other teachers. Today the political ideologies represented by the state are responsible for the killing of people. And they claim that what they are doing is the result of some great revolution that they had started. Revolution is nothing but the revaluation of our values. It does not mean anything. After a while it settles down, and that is why they are talking of Glasnost there [in the Soviet Union]. But it does not really mean anything there. Gorbachev is going to create a hundred Punjabs in that country.

Q: When you use term 'nature', what exactly do you mean?

U.G.: The whole thing that is there. The life forms around: the assemblage of life around this planet. You are not different from all that.

Q: What is creating that assemblage? You say that there is a purpose.

U.G.: No. I am not saying that there is a purpose. You are saying that there is a purpose. It may not have any purpose at all. Your question implies that there must be some reason for all that. What I see is what is happening here and now. But you want to establish a cause-and-effect relationship between the two events. That is the way logical thinking functions in us. Logic is used by us to win an argument over somebody. That also is a destructive weapon; and when logic fails, there is violence. So to ask the question, "Where have we failed? Why have we taken this wrong turn?" to me has no meaning. But an important question that we have to ask is something else: "Are there any answers? Are there any solutions for our problems?"

Q : We do seem to have a need to search and find something.

U.G.: The body does not want to learn anything or know anything, because it has that intelligence – native, innate intelligence – that helps it to survive. If this body is in a jungle, it will survive; if it doesn't, it's gone. But it will fight to the last. That's just the way the human body is functioning. If there is some danger to it, the body throws in everything that is available and tries to protect itself. If it cannot, it gives in. But in a way the body has no death. The atoms in it are put together and what happens at death is a reshuffling of the atoms. They will be used somewhere else. So the body has no birth or death, because it has no way of experiencing that it is alive or that it will be dead tomorrow.

Q : I think that's a point. I would like to listen on.

U.G.: You call this a table, and that you call a dead corpse: but actually there is life there. You see the decomposition that is taking place in the dead body is a form of life. Of course, that's no consolation to the one who has lost his wife. Please don't get me wrong. When death has provided the basis for the continuity of life, how can you call it death? It's a different matter that it is no consolation to me or to the one who has lost his near and dear one. But you can't say that it [the corpse] is dead. Now they are saying that the hair keeps growing, the nails keep growing, and brain waves continue for a long time even after the so-called clinical death.

That is the reason why now they are trying to define death in the courts - there in France and other countries. They find it so difficult to define death. And now in the United States they have gone one step further. They keep the dead bodies in deep freeze so that one day medical science will come up with a cure for the disease that was responsible for the death of that body. Do you know what they will do? They are not going to leave their money to their children. The money will be blocked and it is going to create a tremendous economic stagnation of the movement of money. It's very strange. They call that cryonics. It's gaining ground there in the United States.

Where do you draw the line between life and death? The definition of death is eluding the legal profession; so far they are unable to define what death is. For all practical purposes we have to consider that it's the same as clinical death. But in nature there is no birth and there is no death. Nothing is ever born, and nothing ever dies. So, if that [idea] is applied to the body, which is not separate from the totality of life around, there is neither death nor birth for it.

I am not talking metaphysics. We don't seem to understand the basic fact that we are not able to control these things at all.

The more we try the more troubles we are creating... I may sound very cynical, but a cynic really a realist. I am not complimenting myself. I am talking of cynics in general. Cynicism will help you to have a healthy look at the way things are going on in the world.

Q: When I said that I wanted to read your book, you said that it was dead. What do you mean?

U.G.: I now call my book *The Mistake of Enlightenment* instead of its real title, *The Mystique of Enlightenment*. It is a mistake I made. I don't have any message to give to the world. Frankly speaking, I really don't know what is there in that or in the second book. What I am saying is valid and true for just this moment. That's why people tell me, "You are contradicting yourself all the time". No, not at all. You see, this statement [I am making now] is contradicted by my next statement; a third statement contradicts the first two statements. A fourth statement contradicts – rather negates than contradicts – the first four, and the fifth one negates the sixth even before it is made! This is done not with the idea of arriving at a positive position; the negation is made for the sake of negation because nothing can be expressed, and you can't say *this* is the truth. There is no such thing as truth. A logically ascertained premise, yes. You can write a book on 'My Search for Truth' or God knows what –'My Experiments with truth'.

Q: But aren't you dealing with certain facts or truths as you experience them? They are true irrespective of the immediate time frame.

U.G.: In this particular time frame, all events are independent, and there is no continuity among them. Each event is an independent frame, but you are linking up all these [frames] and trying to channel the movement of life in a particular direction for your ulterior motives. But actually you have no way of controlling the events. They are outside of you. All you can do is establish a relationship with particular events, or put them all together and create a tremendous structure of thought and philosophy.

What Kind Of A Human Being Do You Want?

Q : We always feel that we have to improve ourselves or find at least a way out of our misery. Everyone thinks that he or she has to change or get to a higher level. What is your view on the matter?

U.G.: The moment we ask the question, "Is there something more to our life than what we are doing?" it sets the whole questioning mechanism going. Unfortunately, what has created this interest in Western nations is the so-called Hippy generation. When they tried drugs, the drugs produced a change in what they called their 'level of consciousness'. For the first time they experienced something outside the area of their normal experiencing structure. When once we experience something extraordinary, which actually it is not, we look around for varieties of experiences....

Q : More...?

U.G.: More and more of the same. That has created a market for all those people from the Eastern countries, India, China, and Japan, to flood into these countries and promise to provide answers for their questions. But actually they are selling shoddy pieces of goods. What people are interested in are not some answers to their problems but some comforters. As I said before, they are selling ice packs to numb the pain and make you feel comfortable. Nobody wants to ask the basic question: What is the real problem? What is it that they want? What are they looking for? And this [situation] is taken advantage of by the people from the east. If there is anything to what they claim (that they have the answers and solutions for the problems that we are all facing today), it doesn't seem to be evident in the countries from where they come. The basic question that the Westerners should throw at them is, "Have your answers helped the people of your countries? Do your solutions operate in your own lives?" Nobody is asking them these questions. The hundred different techniques that they offer to you have not been subjected to test. You don't have any statistical evidence to prove that there is something to what they claim. They exploit the gullibility and credulity of the people. When once you have everything that you need, the material goodies, you look around and ask the question, "Is that all there is to it?" And those people exploit that situation. They don't have any answers for the problems facing us today.

What is responsible for the human tragedy or the malady that we are confronted with to day is that we are interested in maintaining the identities that are created by our culture. We have tremendous faith in the value system that is created by our culture or society or whatever you want to call it. We never question that. We are only interested in fitting ourselves into that value system. It is that demand from the society or culture to fit us all into that value system that is the cause of man's tragedy.

Somewhere along the line there occurred in human consciousness the demand to find out the answer for loneliness, the isolation that human beings suffer from the rest of the species on this planet. I don't even know if there is any such thing as evolution. If there is, somewhere along the line in that evolutionary process man separated or isolated himself from the rest of the creation on this planet. In that isolation, he felt so frightened that he demanded some answers, some comfort, to fill that loneliness, that isolation from the rest of the life around him. Religious thinking was born out of this situation, and it has gone on for centuries. But it has not really helped us to solve the problems created by mankind. Even the political systems that we have today are nothing but the outgrowth of the spiritual, religious thinking of man. Unfortunately they have failed, and a void has been created. There has been a total failure of our political and economic ideologies.

There is a tremendous danger facing mankind today. The void created by the failure of all these ideologies will be taken advantage of by the religious organizations. They will preach and shout that we all have to go back to the great traditions of our own countries. But what has failed for them is not going to help us to solve our problems.

When some psychologists and scientists came to see me, I made this very clear to them, "You have come to the end of your tether. If you want answers for your problems, you have to find them within your own framework and not look elsewhere, especially the ancient dead cultures of the past". Going back or looking back to those systems and techniques that have failed us is only going to put us on a wrong track, on a merry-go-round.

Q : That's true. A lot of people are looking back to the past, as if the answers would be there.

U.G.: The situation that we are facing today is only the result of the past, and if we are looking back to the past we are already dead. We have no future at all as long as we try to get the answers from the past that is dead. Anybody who says, "Look back or go back", has no answers to offer us. The future is blocked if someone tells us, "You have to look back", because it is the past that has put us in the present awkward situation. But we are not ready to brush the whole thing aside.

Q : So, all the techniques, the ancient techniques of meditation, Yoga, Tantra, Zen Buddhism, Catholicism, you name it – have they all failed?

U.G.: All of them have totally failed. Otherwise we wouldn't be where we are today. If there were anything to their claims, we would have created a better and happier world. But we are not ready to accept the fact that it is they that are responsible for creating the sorry mess that we are all facing today.

Q : If you look at the political systems like fascism or communism they are very much like a religion.

U.G.: They have their own Church, their own Bible and …

Q : What I find very interesting is that even our procurators have left the church. They have had the big temples,

accepted the same hierarchies as in the church of the middle ages, but all of them have crumbled and still there are millions of victims.

U.G.: We are partly responsible for this situation because we want to be victimized by them. What is the point in blaming those people? There is no point in blaming ourselves either because it is a two-way game: we play the game and they play the game. And playing games is all that we are doing. We are used to patting our own backs and telling ourselves, "God is in the far heavens and all is right with the world". It is very comforting to believe that we are going to do something extraordinary in the future. What we are left with is the hope; and we live in hope and die in hope. What I say doesn't sound promising, but it's a fact.

Q : We keep hoping.

U.G.: That's a very comforting thing - to hope that the future is going to be a marvelous thing and tremendously different from what it has been all these years. But we are not doing anything to create something new.

Q : No, no. We just hope...

U.G.: It is just a rehash of the past, the dead past. We only give new names and put new labels. But basically and essentially it [the religious teaching] has not helped us and it is not going to help us. It is not a question of replacing our ideas with new ideas, our thoughts with new thoughts, our beliefs with new beliefs, for the whole belief structure is very important to us. We do not want to free ourselves from this illusion. If we free ourselves from one illusion, we always replace it with another. If we brush aside or drop one belief, we will always replace that belief with another belief.

Q : Immediately?

U.G.: Immediately. The fact is that we don't want to be free. What is responsible for our problems is the fear of losing what we have and what we know. All these therapies, all these techniques, religious or otherwise, are only perpetuating the agony of man. It is very comforting for people to believe that somehow, through some miracle, they are going to be freed from the problems that they are confronted with today. There is no way out of this because we are all wholly and solely responsible for the problems that we have created for ourselves and for others.

Q : If we have created the problems, we are also fighting them

U.G.: Yes. But we are not ready to accept the fact that what has created the problems cannot itself solve them. What we are using to solve our problems is what we call 'thought'. But thought is a protective mechanism. Thought is only interested in maintaining the status quo. We may talk of change, but when actually the time comes for us to change things, we are not ready for it. We insist that change must always be for the better and not for the worse. We have a tremendous faith in the mechanism that has created the problems for us. After all, that is the only instrument that we have at our disposal, and we don't have any other instrument. But actually it cannot help us at all. It can only create problems, but cannot solve them. We are not ready to accept this fact because accepting it will knock out the whole foundation of human culture. We want to replace one system with another. But the whole structure of culture is pushing us in the direction of completely annihilating all that we have built with tremendous care.

We don't want to be free from fear. Anything you do to free yourself from fear is what is perpetuating the fear. Is there any way we can be freed from fear? Fear is something that cannot be handled by thought; it is something living. So we want to put on our gloves and try to touch it, play with it. All that we want to do is to play games with it and talk about freeing ourselves from fear. Or go to this therapist or that, or follow this technique or that. But in that process, what we are actually doing is strengthening and fortifying the very thing that we are trying to be free from, that is, .fear.

Q : We are putting all our energies into [becoming free from] fear and then it grows?

U.G.: If the tremendous amount of energy that we put into solving this problem is released - I say, 'if'-if it is released, what is it that you cannot do? But there is no way you can do anything about it. If you were lucky enough to find yourself in the situation where you are freed from this [fear] and that energy is released, living in this world would be very simple and easy.

Q : So we live in a society based on fear. Even our institutions - police, banks, doctors, insurance, and every thing we have created – are based on fear?

U.G.: Yes, fear. But what is the point in telling ourselves that we are going to be freed from fear? If that fear comes to an end, you will drop dead, Physically! Clinical death will take place! Of course, you and your fear are not two different things. It is comforting to believe that you and fear are not two different things. You are frightened of certain things, or you do not want this or that thing to happen. You want to be free from fear. All this is very comforting, but there is no way you can separate yourself from fear and do anything to free yourself from it. If the fear comes to an end, 'you' as you know yourself, 'you' as you experience yourself, are going to come to an end, and you are not ready for that sort of thing.

The plain fact is that if you don't have a problem, you create one. If you don't have a problem, you don't feel that you are living. So the solutions that we have been offered by the teachers, in whom we have tremendous faith; are not really the solutions. If they were the solutions, the problems wouldn't be there at all. If there were no solutions for the problems, even then the problems wouldn't be there. We would like to live with those problems, and if we are free from one problem, we create another.

Q: Without problems you would be bored, wouldn't you?

U.G.: Boredom is a bottomless pit. There is no way you can be freed from boredom. You love your boredom, but all the time you are trying to free yourself from boredom. As long as you think that there is something more interesting, more purposeful, more meaningful to do than what you are actually doing, you have no way of freeing yourself from boredom. So, it goes on and on. If you don't entertain yourself with a cowboy movie, you might go to a church and pray, or you might go to a temple and pray, or you might want to listen to a holy man telling you all kinds of stories. He will sell you some shoddy piece of goods, "Stand on your head, stand on your shoulders, do this and do that," and you will be all right.

But the basic question which none of us is willing to ask is: what is it that we want? Whether you are in Holland, in America, or in Africa, anywhere, what you are really interested in is the quest for permanent happiness. That is all that we are interested in. all these religious people, the gurus, and the holy men, who are marketing these shoddy pieces of spiritual goods, are telling us that there is some way you can have eternal and permanent happiness. But that doesn't happen. We invest our faith in them so that it gives us hope, and we go on doing the same thing over and over again. And we continue to live in that hope. But it does not help us to get what we are really interested in, namely, to be permanently happy. There is no such thing as permanence at all, let alone permanent happiness.

The quest for permanent happiness is a lost battle; but we are not ready to accept that fact. What we are left with is some moments of happiness and some moments of unhappiness. If we are not ready to accept that situation, and still demand a non-existent permanent happiness, we are not going to succeed.

It is just a question of succeeding, or wanting to be in a permanent state of happiness, but that demand is the enemy of this living organism. The organism is not interested in happiness at all. It is only interested in its survival. What are necessary for the survival of this living organism are its sensory perceptions along with the sensitivity of the senses and nervous system. The moment you find yourself in a happy situation and tell yourself that you are happy; the demand that this happiness should continue for a longer time is bound to be there. And the more you try to prolong that sensation of happiness beyond its natural duration, the more there is danger for this system which is only interested in maintaining its sensitivity. So, there is a battle going on between your demand for permanent happiness and the demand of the body to maintain its sensitivity. You are not going to win this battle; yet you are not ready to give it up.

Q : Does meditation affect the body?

U.G.: You put your body to unnecessary torture.

Q : The body suffers?

U.G.: Yes, the body suffers. It is not interested in your techniques of meditation, which actually are destroying the peace that is already there. It is an extraordinarily peaceful organism. It does not have to do anything to be in a peaceful state. By introducing this idea of a peaceful mind, we set in motion a sort of battle, and the battle goes on and on. But what you feel, what you experience as the peaceful state of mind, is a war-weary state of mind, you want more and more of the same. This creates problems for the body.

Q : And by wanting more of the same, you literally harm the body?

U.G.: Yes, harm the body. And you pay a heavy price.

Q : I want to know whether the body learns on its own for example, when a baby cries, it has no idea of crying.

U.G.: If you let the baby cry it will eventually stop.

Q : Automatically...?

U.G.: Automatically. The baby will be exhausted. The baby cries because it is trying to express through that crying some discomfort. But we don't understand what the discomfort is. We are interested only in our comfort, and that is why we try to stop the baby from crying. We have created a neurotic situation for the baby from the very start. We don't have the energy to deal with the problems of living beings, and the child is a living thing. It would be more interesting to learn from children, than try to teach them how to behave, how to live and how to function.

Q : How to suppress...

U.G.: Because we suppress everything in us, we want to suppress everything in the growing child. We have already created a problem for the child instead of finding out what actually is his problem. We don't have the energy to deal with the problems of children. We curse them and then we push them to fit into this framework of ours, created by us for our own reasons.

This is what we call culture. Culture is not anything mysterious. It is your way of life and your way of thinking. All the other cultural activities we consider to be very creative are part and parcel of your way of living and thinking. And your way of thinking is the thing that has created all these problems for you. There is no way you can free yourself from the problems created by thinking except by setting in motion another kind of thinking. But that cannot be of help.

Actually there are no thoughts there [within you]. Thoughts are not self-generated. They are not spontaneous. We never look at a thought. What is there is *about* thought but not thought itself. We are ready to question that and face the fact that thoughts are not spontaneous. They come from outside – outside in the sense that when there is a sensory response to a stimulus, we translate that sensation within the framework of our knowledge, and tell ourselves that that [the translation] is the sensation. You recognize the sensation and give a name to it. That is what memory is all about. What is there is only memory. Where is that memory?

Really, nobody knows where memory is. You can say that it is in the neurons. When once the sensory perceptions activate the senses that are involved, they in their turn, activate the memory cells. We capture every movement there [in the sensation] within the framework of the memory structure and translate it.

Naturally, memory is born out of our demand to isolate ourselves, censor the sensory perceptions and filter them in order to maintain the status quo and continuity of the movement of our knowledge. We may talk of freeing ourselves from knowledge. But whatever we are doing is not freeing us from the movement of knowledge. On the contrary, it is strengthening and fortifying the very thing that we are trying to be free from.

Q : Your statements seem to resemble what the quantum physicists tell us. Our thinking about the universe is very limited.

U.G.: We are creating the universe ourselves. We have no way of looking at the universe at all. The model that we see is created by our thought. Even the scientists who say that they are observing certain things have actually no way of observing anything except through the mirror of their own thinking. The scientist is influencing what you are looking at. Whatever theories he comes up with are only theories; they are not facts to him. Even if you are looking at the object physically, without the interference of thought and without translating what you are looking at, the physical looking is affecting the object that you are looking at. Actually there is no way you can capture, contain and give expression to what you are looking at. You dare not look at anything. Scientists can come up with all kinds of theories, hundreds and hundreds of them. You can only reward them with Nobel prizes or give them some prestigious awards, and that is all that they are interested in. But, are we ready to accept the fact that there is no way that you can look at anything? You are not looking at anything at all. Even the physical looking is influenced by your thought. There is no way you can look at anything without the use of the knowledge that you have of what you are looking at. In fact, it is that [the knowledge] that is creating the object. It is your thinking that is creating the observer. So this whole talk of the observer and the observed is balderdash. There is neither the 'observer' nor the 'observed'. [The talk of] the 'perceiver' and the 'perceived', the 'seer' and the 'seen' is all bosh and nonsense. These themes are good for endless metaphysical discussions. There is no end to such discussions. And to believe that there is an observation without the observer is a lot of baloney.

Q : Hogwash...

U.G.: Hogwash and hot air...[Laughter] There is no way you can look at anything without the 'looker', who is the product of this thinking.

Q : This week there is going to be an important meeting here. Important scientists from all over the world from different disciplines – people from the spiritual world and the world of industry and economics – are for the first time coming together to talk about the similarities among their respective disciplines instead of differences. All of them now seem to feel that they should support each other in stead of focussing their energies only on differences and the compartments that they create in their minds.

U.G.: First of all, the scientists, by looking or asking for help from all these religious people, are committing the biggest of all blunders. They have come to the end of their tether. If they have problems in their systems they have to solve them by and for themselves. These religious people have no answers for the problems created by the scientific thinking of man. I do not know if by coming together and exchanging their views or giving speeches they are going to achieve anything. I may sound very cynical when I say that nothing is going to come out of it except that they will make speeches and feel comfortable that they are trying to understand each other's point of view. When you say something to someone, he will say that that is *your* point of view. But he does not realize that his also is a point of view. So, how can there be any communication between two people who have different points of view? The whole purpose of the conversation or dialogue is only to convert the other man to *your* point of view. If you have no point of view, there is no way he can convince or convert you to his point of view. So this dialogue is between two points of view and there is no way you can reconcile them.

The conference would be very interesting [Laughs]. They can all come together, talk about that [what is common to their different disciplines] and exchange their views, and that would be that. It would be something like the United Nations. (The United Nations is the biggest joke of this century. If each one is trying to assert his own rights there, how can there be a United Nations?) The problem is that thought creates frontiers everywhere. That's all it can do.

Q : Differences...?

U.G.: Differences. So it is thought that has created the world; and you draw lines on this planet, "This is my country, that is your country". So, how can there be unity between two countries? The very thing that is creating the frontiers and differences cannot be the means to bridge the different viewpoints. It is an exercise in futility.

Q : Yes, true.

U.G.: I may sound very cynical when I point this out. But they know in their hearts that nothing will come out [of their deliberations]. We are not ready to accept the fact that thought can only create problems. That instrument cannot be of any help to us.

The talk of intuition and insight is another illusion. Every insight you have is born out of your thinking. The insights strengthen and fortify the very thing you are trying to be free from. All insights, however extraordinary they may be, are worthless. You can create a tremendous structure of thought from your own discovery, which you call insight. But that insight is nothing but the result of your own thinking, the permutations and combinations of thought. Actually there is no way you can come up with anything original there. There is no thought that you can call your own. I don't have any thoughts which I call my own - not one thought, not one word, not one experience. Everything comes from outside. If I have to experience anything, I have to depend upon the knowledge that is put in here. Otherwise there is no way you can experience anything. What you do not know, you cannot experience. There is no such thing as a new experience at all.

I even question the idea of consciousness. They may not be any such thing as consciousness at all, let alone the subconscious, the unconscious, and all the other levels of consciousness. How do you become conscious of a thing? You become conscious of a thing only through your memory. First, you recognize it. And the recognition and naming are all that are there. You can trick yourself into the belief that recognition and naming are two different things. But actually they are not. The very fact that you recognize something as an object even without naming it means that you 7already know about it. The memory that has captured it says that it is an object. The talk about recognition without naming is a very clever way of playing a game. It is only sharpening your intellect. Actually you are not trying to understand what the problem is or how to deal with it.

Q : So what do you call instinct? Is it another idea in the mind?

U.G.: It is another idea invented by thought. Whatever we experience is thought-induced.

Q : There cannot be anything else?

U.G.: What you don't know you cannot experience. To experience a thing you have to 'know'.

Q : For instance, when people from a jungle in Africa were shown their photograph they could not recognize them selves at all.

U.G.: The re cognition of yourself as an entity is possible only through the help of the knowledge [you have about yourself]. We start this process with children. You tell a child: "Show me your teeth, show me your nose, show me your ears, or tell me your name". That is where identity starts. The constant use of memory to maintain that identity is the situation we find ourselves in. We do not want that identity to come to an end. We do everything possible to maintain it. But the effort to maintain your identity is wearing you out.

The constant use of memory to maintain our identity will put us all ultimately in a state where we are forced to give up. When someone gives up the attempt to fit him or herself into the value system, you call that person crazy. He (or she, as the case may be) has given up. Some people don't want to fit into that framework. We push them to be functional. The more we push them to be functional, the crazier they become. Actually, we are pushing them to suicide.

The alternatives before mankind are either suicide or the fashionable disease, what we call Alzheimer's disease. Whether the disease occurs due to damaged tissue in the brain or through the use of aluminum vessels, as some claim, they really don't know yet. But this seems to be the fate of mankind. These are the only ways your identity can be destroyed. It is amazing how thousands and thousands of people are affected by it. Even middle-aged people are affected. The constant use of memory to maintain your identity, whether you are asleep, awake or dreaming, *is* what is going to destroy not only the human species, but also all forms of life on this planet. It is not a happy prophecy. I am not a prophet. I am not prophesying anything. But from what we know and what is happening today, that seems to be the fate of mankind.

Q : Do you think that the discovery of the laws of nature and the economous money that is invested in it will ultimately help mankind?

U.G.: Even if we discover the laws of nature, for whatever reason we are interested in doing so, ultimately they are used to destroy everything that nature has created. This propaganda that the planet is in danger is media hype. Everybody has in fact forgotten about it. Actually it is not the planet that is in danger, but we are in danger. We are not ready to face this situation squarely. We must not look for answers in the past or in the great heritage of this or that nation. And we must not look to the religious thinkers.

They don't have any answers. If the scientists look to the religious leaders for their solutions, they are committing the biggest blunder. The religious people put us all on the wrong track, and there is no way you can reverse the process.

Q : What do you think we should do then?

U.G.: I am not here to save mankind or prophesy that we are all heading toward a disaster. I am not talking of an Armageddon, nor am I prophesying that there is going to be any paradise on this planet. It is the idea of a paradise, the idea of creating a heaven on this earth, which has turned this beautiful paradise that we already have on this planet into a hell. We are solely responsible for what is happening. And the answers for our problems cannot come from the past and its glory, or from the great religious teachers of mankind. Those teachers will naturally claim that you have failed and that they have the answers for the problems that we are confronted with today. I don't think that they have any answers. We have to find out the answers, if there are any, for ourselves and by ourselves.

Q : I have read somewhere, "You image is your best friend".

U.G.: [Laughs] That's a sales pitch; it's very interesting. In fact, it's the other way around: the image we have is responsible for our problems. What, after all, is the world? The world is the relationship between two individuals. But that relationship is based on the foundation of "What do I get out of a relationship?" Mutual gratification is the basis of all relationships. If you don't get what you want out of a relationship, it goes sour. What there is in the place of what you call a 'loving relationship' is hate. When everything fails, we play the last card in the pack, and that is 'love'. But love is fascist in its nature, in its birth, in its expression and in its action. It cannot do us any good. We may talk of love but it doesn't mean anything. The whole music of our age is all around that song, "Love, Love, Love..."

Q : "I love you..."[Laughter]

U.G.: You want to assure yourself and assure your friend that you love. Why do you need all the time the assurance that you love the other individual?

Q : There are no questions, according to you?

U.G.: There are no questions but only answers. We already have the answers. I don't have any questions of any kind. How come you have questions? The only kind of questions I have are ones like, "How does this microphone work?" I ask that because I don't know its working. I have questions only as to how these mechanical things are operating. For living situations we have no answers at all. You cannot apply this mechanical, technical know-how, which we have acquired through repeated study, to solve the problems of living.

We are not really interested in solving the latter kind of problems. We do not know a thing about life. Nobody knows. You can only give a definition. What we know is that our living has become terribly boring. We want a way out of that situation. So we have invented all kinds of ways of entertaining ourselves, whether it is the church or politics or entertainment or music or Disneyland. Yet there is no end to that at all. You need more and more. There comes a time when you will not be able to find anything to free yourself from this boredom of life.

Q : Do you like television?

U.G.: Yes, I do watch television. I turn off the sound and watch the movement only. I like to watch the commercials because most of the commercials are more interesting than the programmes. If people can fall for the commercials, they can fall for anything that these religious people are selling today in the market. How can you fall for those commercials? But they are very interesting. It is not the commercials nor what they are selling that interests me, but the technique of salesmanship. They are amazing and more interesting – I am fascinated by those techniques. I am not influenced by what they are selling. If they had customers like me they would be soon out of business. I don't buy anything they are selling.

Q : So sales pitch is the main literature in America?

U.G.: Yes. I don't know how long they can go on like that. But now others have also copied that. Even in India they have commercials.

Q : Soon they will have it in Russia and Eastern Europe.

U.G.: That's what has happened in Russia. It is not your [American] ideas of democracy or freedom that have won the country over to your side. It was Coca Cola, I think, in China, and Pepsi Cola in Russia. Why do you have to sell organically grown potato chips in Russia? I want to know. They have also opened a McDonald's there. That's all that the West can offer to them. That it how it [commercialism] is spreading. If America survives, if we survive, and if we don't destroy ourselves through our own idiotic ways of living and thinking, the American way of life is going to be the way of life. Even in the third world countries including India they have these supermarkets. They are very innovative, the Americans. So, it [commercialism] is spreading all over.

Q : The problem with the supermarkets is that people develop a thieving tendency.

U.G.: I am not against stealing, but I tell people, "Steal but don't get caught". [Laughter] It is stupid to get caught. All the politicians, the whole government machinery thrives on stealing, promising something which they cannot deliver. It is amazing that we have tremendous faith in all these religious people who cannot deliver the goods. In a business deal, if your partner refuses or fails to deliver the goods, that is the end of the business relationship. But here in the area of religion they can get away with just promising something. They don't deliver the goods at all. How we can fall for that kind of a thing is beyond me. The whole con game has gone on for centuries. But why do we allow ourselves to be conned by those con men? There is not a single exception. All these spiritual teachers of mankind from the very beginning have conned themselves into the belief that they have the answers, the solutions for mankind.

Q : This is from Buddha to Jesus, to...

U.G.: Yes, yes, all of them. And all those who are in the market place today.

Q : And in the past...?

U.G.: And in the past, in the present and in the future. [Laughter…]

Q : It means their goods did not work?

U.G.: No, not at all. They cannot deliver the goods. They only give us hope. As I said at the beginning, we live in hope and die in hope.

Q : We learn something during our upbringing and we believe it. Would you say our minds are programmed?

U.G.: The basic question that we all have to ask is: What kind of human being you want in this world?

Q : Or where we want to be?

U.G.: Or where we want to be. Society is trying to create the human beings. That is what society has done. You and I have been created by the society, solely and wholly to maintain its continuity, its status quo. You have no way of establishing your own individuality. You have to use that [society and all its heritage] to experience yourself as an entity and to function in this world. If you don't accept the reality of the world as it is imposed on us, you will end up in the loony bin. But we *have* to accept that. The moment we question the reality of what has been imposed on us we are in trouble.

What I am saying is that you have to answer this question for yourself, "What do we want"? This was my problem. I asked myself, "Is there anything I want other than what *they* wanted me to want? Is there anything I want to think other than what *they* wanted me to think?" Nobody could help me in this area, and that was my problem. I had no way of finding out an answer. Wanting not to want what the others wanted me to want was also a want. It never occurred to me that this was no different from all the other wants. Somewhere along the line the question somehow disappeared; I don't know how. What I am left with is something that I have no way of experiencing, and no way of communicating or transmitting to anybody.

That is the difficulty I have when I meet people. I have no way of communicating the certainty that occurred in me that there is no way I can understand anything through the instrument which I used for years and years, the instrument being the intellect. It has not helped me to solve any problem. No understanding is possible through that instrument, but that is the most powerful instrument and the only instrument we have. You cannot brush that aside and throw it away. But that is not the instrument, and there is no other instrument. The talk of intuition only puts us on a merry-go-round. It doesn't lead us anywhere.

Q: What do they mean when they say that the 'heart' understands?

U.G.: You want to know? You are making this assumption that to have a 'heart' is better than to use your head. The whole religious thinking is built on the foundation of having a good heart and giving supremacy and importance to it, and not to what your 'head' is doing. But what I want to say is that the heart is there only to pump blood. It is not interested in your kindly deeds. If you indulge in kindly deeds, doing good unto others, having a good 'heart', you will only create problems for the heart. It is the beginning of your cardiac problems! That's going to be a real problem. It is your kindly deeds that are responsible for the cardiac arrests and heart failures, and not any [mal] functioning of the heart. The tremendous importance that we have given to the 'heart' is totally irrelevant. To make a distinction between the 'head' and the 'heart' is interesting, but in the long run it is not going to help us.

The reality of the matter is that even your feelings are thoughts. If you tell yourself that you are happy, you are translating that sensation of happiness within the framework of the knowledge you have. So that too is a thought. There are no pure feelings at all. What you are stuck with are only thoughts, and those thoughts are put in there by your culture.

We have also invented this idea of freeing yourself from thoughts. How are you going to succeed in freeing yourself from thoughts? It is only through the help of *another* thought. Actually there are no thoughts there at all. What you find there is that the very question that we ask ourselves and ask others, namely, "Is there a thought?" is itself born out of thought. If you want to look at thought and find out for yourself if there is any such thing as thought, what you will find there is [a thought] *about* thought but *not* thought itself. So we really don't know if there are any thoughts, let alone good thoughts or bad thoughts. And there is no thinker there either. The thinker, the non-existent thinker, comes into being only when you use your thought to achieve your goals. It doesn't matter what the goal is, or whether it is material or spiritual. When once you use thoughts to achieve a goal, we create a non-existent thinker. But actually there is no thinker. There is nobody who is talking now. There is only 'talking', there is only 'seeing', there is only 'listening'. But the moment you translate that listening, interpret it in terms of the framework of your reference point; you have created a problem. Its [thought's] interest is to interpret and translate. It helps only to strengthen and fortify the very thing, which you are trying to free yourself from.

Q : It is an addiction.

U.G.: Yes, it is like a dog chasing its own tail; or like your trying to overcome your own shadow. But you never ask how this shadow is cast.

Q : How is the shadow cast?

U.G.: [Laughs] With the help of the light. Your wanting to over-take your own shadow is an exercise in futility. We are not taking anything seriously. This is all frivolous.

Q : I have heard that time is money.

U.G.: Because money is the most important factor in our lives. They say that money is the root cause of all evil. But actually it is not the root cause of evil; it is the root cause of our existence, of our survival. I sometimes say that if you worship that god, the money god, you will be amply rewarded. If you worship the other God – whether he exists or not is anybody's guess – you will be stripped of everything you have, and he will leave you naked in the streets. It is better to worship the money god.

Q : Money god...

U.G.: Money god. And you will be amply rewarded. Tell me one person who is not thinking of money. Not one person on this planet. Even the holy ones who talk about their indifference to money are concerned about it. How do you think they will get ninety-two Rolls Royces? You try and buy one Rolls Royce car;

you will know how difficult it is. For the religious people it is easy because other people deny themselves and give their money to them. So you can be rich at another man's expense. How much money you need is a different matter. Each one has to draw his own line. But when once your goals and needs are the same, then the problem is very simple.

Q : The goal and needs are...?

U.G.: ...The goals and needs are the same. You have no goals beyond your needs or beyond your means.

Q : So you stay more or less here, in this moment, and deal with what happens right now.

U.G.: When once that becomes a reality in your life, it becomes very simple to live in this world, the complex and complicated world created by us all. We are responsible for this world. When once this demand to change yourself into something better, something other than what you actually are, is not there, the demand to change the world also comes to an end. I don't see anything wrong with the world. What is wrong with this world? The world can't be anything different from what we are. If there is a war going on within us, we cannot accept a peaceful world around us. We will certainly create war. You may say that it all depends upon who is responsible for the war. It is simply a point of view as to who is calling another a warmonger and oneself the 'peace-monger'. The peace-mongers and the warmongers sail in the same boat. It is something like the pot calling the kettle black, or the other way around: the kettle calling the pot black.

Q : These proverbs or folks sayings are quite to the point.

U.G.: Yes, they are to the point. They are really the utterances of wise men who have observed the reality of the world exactly the way it is.

Q : There is an old expression that says, "There is nothing to understand".

U.G.: There is nothing to understand. How that understanding dawned on me, I really don't know. The understanding that this instrument [the intellect] is really not the instrument to understand anything is something that cannot be communicated. This instrument is only interested in perpetuating itself through what it calls 'understanding', which in reality are its own machinations. It is only sharpening itself to maintain its own continuity. When once you know that it is the instrument and that there is no other instrument, then there is nothing more to understand.

Q : It is actually quite simple.

U.G.: Yes, very simple. But this very simple fact of our life, of our existence, is something, which the complex structure that we have created is not ready to accept, because its very simplicity is going to shatter the complexity. What, after all, is evolution, if there is any such thing as evolution? It is the simple becoming complex. The complex structure is not ready to face this situation - the very simplicity of the whole process. When once that is understood, the whole theory of evolution collapses. Maybe there is such a thing as evolution. We really don't know for sure. When once you accept that there is an evolution in the life around, you put the same thing in the spiritual realm and say that there is also spiritual progress. You will say, "I am more evolved than my neighbour – spiritually speaking, more evolved than my fellow beings". That makes us feel superior to all.

Q : I am more spiritual than you.

U.G.: I am more spiritual than my fellow beings… So the very complexity, which we are responsible for, is not ready to leave that simple thing alone, to leave it simple.

Q : If we accept 'what is'…

U.G.: That is a very misleading phrase, to accept 'what is'. It is very interesting to talk about 'what is', but you cannot describe that 'what is' in any manner. And you cannot leave 'what is' as it is. You cannot even complete the sentence and say, 'what is *is*'. But we don't stop there. We build a tremendous structure, the fantasy structure, romantic structure, on 'what is' and talk about love, bliss, beatitude, or immensity.

Q : We are stuck in words and ideas.

U.G.: We dare not leave that 'what is' alone. It implies that you are still grappling with what you romantically phrase as 'what is'. It is like dealing with the unknown. There is no such thing as the unknown. The known is still trying to make the unknown part of the known. It is a game that we play. That is how we fool ourselves in our approach to problems. All our positive approaches have failed. And we have invented what is called the 'negative approach'. But the negative approach is still interested in the same goal that the positive approach is interested in. What is necessary for us is to free ourselves from the goal. When once we are freed from the goal [of solving problems], the question of whether it is a positive approach or a negative approach does not even arise.

Q : So in nature the positive and the negative don't exist at all?

U .G.: They don't exist at all. If they do, they exist in the same frame. That is what these scientists are talking about. If you observe the universe, there is chaos in it. The moment you say there is chaos; in the same frame, there is also order. So, you cannot, for sure, say that there is order or chaos in the universe. Both of them are occurring simultaneously. That is the way the living organism also operates. The moment thought is born; it cannot stay there. Thought is matter. When once the matter that is necessary for the survival of the living organism is created, that matter becomes part of energy. Similarly life and death are simultaneous processes. It is thought that has separated and created the two points of birth and death. Thought has created this space and this time. But actually, birth and death are simultaneous processes.

You cannot say whether you are born or dead. You cannot say that you are alive or dead. But if you ask me the question, "Are you alive?" I would certainly say, "I am alive". So my answer is the common knowledge you and I have about how a living being functions. That is how I say that I am a living being and not a dead person. But we give tremendous importance to these ideas. We sit and discuss them everlastingly and produce a tremendous structure of thought around them.

Q : Shall I go back to my original question about change in human beings?

U.G.: Yes, what kind of human being do you want? Culture, society, or whatever you want to call it, has placed before us the model of a perfect being, which is the model of the great spiritual teachers of mankind. But it is not possible for every one of us to be like that. You are unique in your own way. There is no way you can copy those men. That is where we have created the tremendous problem for the whole of mankind.

Q : These people want to be like the Buddha...

U.G.: Like the Buddha or like Jesus. Thank God, you cannot be like Jesus because there is one and only one Jesus.

Q : Yes, you are right.

U.G.: To that extent many people are saved from trying to be like Jesus. But in India they accept Jesus also as one of the great teachers of mankind. They tell themselves and others that Jesus is there to enable you to become a Christ and not a Christian. But that is not acceptable by the Christians, because it destroys the whole foundation of the church; it destroys the whole foundation of Christianity. If there was a Christ, you have to accept his word when he says, "I am the way, I am the truth, and I am the life. Through me you will reach the eternal Father". That statement, whether he made it or someone else put it in his mouth, has created the foundation for the whole church. You cannot exonerate the leaders of the church and only blame the followers for the sorry mess of things they have created for us.

The whole ethical culture and everything that we have created to rule ourselves with are born out of the thinking of man. We are not ready to accept the fact that nature probably is interested in creating only perfect species and not perfect individuals. Nature does not use any model. It creates something; then it destroys it, and creates something else. The comparative process characteristic of thinking seems to be absent.

So what kind of human being do you want? The whole ethical culture that is built by us to shape the actions of man has totally failed. The commandment, "Thou shall not steal", has not helped. If you want to free a human being from thieving tendencies we have to find some other way of doing it, whatever your reasons are to free him from those tendencies. Probably you have to find a drug to change the chemistry of those who have the tendencies.

Q : There is a biotechnology coming out...

U.G.: But there is also a danger, a tremendous danger. When once you perfect genetic engineering and transform human beings through chemical means or genetic engineering, you will certainly hand the means over to the state. Then it becomes easy for the state to control people without brainwashing them. Brainwashing takes decades and decades, probably even centuries. The fact that we have outlawed murder has not put an end to murder. It's only on the increase. I am not for a moment saying that if murder is not outlawed, there will be fewer murders. In spite of outlawing murder, murder is on the increase. Why is that so? Your argument will be that if it is not outlawed, there will be more murders. But I am not impressed by that logic at all. Why is murder on the increase?

Q : Because you are putting energy into it.

U.G.: You put energy into it. The moment you condemn certain things; people have ways and means of overcoming them....

Q : Isn't it true when we are against something or trying to get rid of something, it will keep growing?

U.G.: We are not ready to accept that. Whatever we are doing to free ourselves from the problems that we have created is what is perpetuating them.

Q : But when there is perfection...

U.G.: No. That perception is the enemy of this body.

Q : It is the enemy of the body...?

U.G.: The body is not interested in your perceptions. It is not interested in learning anything from you or knowing anything from you. All the intelligence that is necessary for this living organism is already there. Our attempts to teach this body, or make it function differently from the way it is programmed by nature, *are* what are responsible for the battle that is going on. There is a battle between what is put in by culture and what is inherent there in the body.

The body knows what is good for itself. It can survive and it *has* survived for millions of years. It is not concerned about your pollution or your ecology, or about the way you are treating it. What it is concerned with is in its own survival. And it *will* survive. There is no doubt about it. When the time comes, it will probably flush the whole thing [the cultural input] out of its system. That would be the luckiest day for mankind. That is something that cannot be achieved through any volition or effort, or through the help of any teacher who says that there are ways and means of freeing you from the stranglehold of your thoughts.

Q : Does that mean that the scientists who are coming next week need to recognize the fact that there is no way out.

U.G.: If they could, then they wouldn't give any solutions, and wouldn't offer anything. There is no way out. The solution for their problems is to accept the fact that there is no way out. And out of that [acceptance] something can come.

Q : Even if you understand the right or wrong of the matter...

U.G.: It is not a question of calling it right or wrong. There is no way out. Anything you do to get out of this trap, which you yourself have created, is strengthening and fortifying it.

Q : Yes, exactly.

U.G.: So, you are not ready to accept the fact that you have to give up. A complete total surrender. I don't want to use that word 'surrender', because it has certain mystical overtones. It is a state of hopelessness, which says that there is no way out of this situation. Any movement, in any direction, on any level, is taking you away from that. Maybe something can happen there, we don't know. But even that hope that something will happen is still a hope.

Q : So you give up completely?

U.G.: You see, giving up something in the hope of getting something else in its place is not really giving up. There is nothing to give up there. The very idea of giving up, the very idea of denying certain things to yourself, is in the hope of getting something else.

Q : Sometimes it so happens that when you give up everything without any expectations the problem gets automatically resolved.

U.G.: Yes. This happens to all those who are working out some mathematical or scientific problem. They go to sleep when they are exhausted, and that gives some time for the mechanism that is involved, and you are ready with the answer. It is not some miraculous thing. You give some time for the computer to work out a solution to your problem. On its own it comes out with the answer, but only if there is an answer. If there is no answer then that is the end of the story.

Q : So basically this means you can't do anything?

U.G.: You can't do a thing; yet you don't stop there. All those who say that you can do something are telling you that there is a way out.

Q : Yet you can't sit down without doing anything. The problem is that one may become a Zombie...

U.G.: Not at all. You cannot stop the movement of life.

Q : It goes on...

U.G.: You don't try to channel the movement of life in any particular direction to produce any special results.

Q : So you let go? It is very difficult to frame questions because of the problem of language.

U.G.: Our language structure is such that there is no way you can be free from a dualistic approach to problems. I don't want to use the word 'dualistic' because it again has religious connotations.

Q : What is the relationship between words and reality?

U.G.: None. There is nothing beyond words.

Q : But there are memories.

U.G.: Memory is playing a trick with itself because it tells you that it is not the words that you are left with but something other than the words. But the fact that you remember something of what has gone on between us both implies that the impact of the words is translated by memory, which then tells you that it [the memory] is something other than the words.

Q : A psychologist had once said that the memory field is outside the body.

U.G.: That's what I am saying too. Thoughts are outside the field of the body. I don't think that the brain has anything to do with creativity at all. The brain is just a reactor and a container.

Q : A type of memory?

U.G.: What is memory after all? Nobody knows what it is. You can give a definition as a student of psychology. "Memory is the mental response of recalling a specific thing at a specific time". That was the definition that I had learned in psychology textbooks.. But that is too silly a definition because nobody knows what memory is or where it is located. You can examine the brain after you are dead, after I am dead. But you won't see any difference between the brain of a genius and the brain of a low-grade moron. So we really don't know. A scientist comes out with some theory. You may award him a Nobel Prize. Then someone else comes along, blasts his theory and offers another one. Every leap year there is a new theory.

Q : There is also this talk about the morphogenetic field.

U.G.: But that implies that there is something that you can do with the genes.

Q : Do you understand that term?

U.G. : Of course, I do. I know something about the morphogenetic theory. The whole motivation, if I may use that word, behind all this is that you still want to do something, change something. All the research projects are geared to the idea of learning something about the way memory operates and the way the human body is functioning, so that you can then apply what you have discovered, which is very limited in the first place. It [the subject matter of life, the human body, and memory] is such a vast thing that what you know is only a teeny-weeny bit of what there is. Your only interest is to bring about a change. But we are not ready to accept that there is nothing to be changed. Scientific discoveries are microscopic compared to the destructive use we put them to. What we have discovered of the laws of nature is only used for destructive purposes. We have tremendous weapons of destruction today. If the church has these instruments of destruction, I don't think you and I would be here, much less evolve any other way of dealing with our problems and our lives.

Q : Yes, indeed! There was a time when the church was full of powers...

U.G.: But now it is trying to again step in.

Q : Yes, especially in the Eastern European countries...

U.G.: Yes. The Russian Orthodox Church will have another heyday. That's all right, but all these countries from East to West,

North to South, will step in now. I am glad that there are more enlightened people in the West that in India. The Westerners are not talking of just their Christianity. They claim that they are enlightened people, and they are out to enlighten the vast millions. Maybe one of these days all these people will go to India and try to enlighten the people there.

Q : Yes, in India. You are right...

U.G.: I won't be surprised.

Q : We have already great enlightened Americans...

U.G.: Yes, lots of them. It's good in a way because that has put an end to all those teachers coming from the Eastern countries to exploit the people here in the West. It would be interesting if you import all that religious stuff into these countries and give your high-tech and technology to those third world countries. They will most probably be able to compete with you in the West. [Laughter]

Q : You are always at Bangalore?

U.G.: No. I don't have any abode of my own. I spend four months in India, four months in Europe, mostly in Switzerland, and four months in the United States.

Q : Are you married or you are a bachelor?

U.G.: I was married in the past, and my wife has been dead for I don't know how long, twenty-three years.

Q : Twenty-three years?

U.G.: She has been dead. I think she has been dead for twenty-seven years. My children are there, but my contact with them is very limited. They visit me. But when they start talking about their lives and try to relate to me in a sentimental way, I feel funny.

Q : Do you live India or...?

U.G.: No. I don't live in any particular place. I am here today, and tomorrow I will be in America, or God knows where. I have no fixed abode. I have no tangible means of livelihood. That is the definition of a vagabond. Mine is a sort of gypsy life. I have just enough money to travel and take care of my physical needs. So, I don't depend upon anyone. The world does not owe a living to me. Why should the world feed me? I am not contributing anything to the world. Why should the world feed me and take care of me?

Q : If people want to come and listen to your answering of questions...

U.G.: No, no. I don't want many people. I am trying to avoid all the seekers. Here they have invented the word 'finders'. 'Finders' means those who have found the truth. I don't want seekers. And if there are any finders, they don't need my help.

Q : Yes, that's right.

U.G.: By allowing myself to be surrounded by those people, I am inadvertently participating in the illusion that by carrying on a dialogue or a conversation with me they are getting something.

So lately I have been discouraging people. Even if they just come and sit around me, I try to point out the ridiculous nature of this get together. I try to finish it by saying, "Nice meeting you all". But still they don't go. They would sit with me for hours and hours. Even if I get up and go away, they would be still there sitting and talking. They would be talking about what I did or did not say, or what they thought I had said. [Laughter] It's happening everywhere and in India too. But there we are used to this kind of thing.

Q : And you even say to people, "Goodbye, and don't come back".

U.G.: Still they keep coming back. I have been very emphatic these days saying that I don't want to see Krishnamurti's 'widows'. Most of those who come to see me are the followers of J. Krishnamurti. I mean J. Krishnamurti freaks, and also the 'widows' of Rajneesh, and all kind of religious buffs - of all shapes, sizes, and colours. Unless they have some sort of background in all this, they can't be interested in this kind thing. They come to receive some confirmation from me about what they are interested in. But they find that they are not getting anything from me. Still they continue to come. You have no idea of how many thousands and thousands of people have passed through the precincts of my homes in India, America, Europe, Australia, and New Zealand. Some of them are intelligent enough to realize that they are not going to get anything from me and that there is no point in hanging around me. But still I have a few friends, whom I call my Enemies Number One, Two, Three, Four, Five etc. [Laughter]. They hang around me, but I don't think they expect anything from me. I am not so sure that they don't expect anything from me. They are not ready to accept what I emphasize and assert all the time: that whatever has happened to me has happened despite everything I did. Some friends who have been with me for years say that they still have the hope that they are going to get something from me. This, in short, is the story of my life. [Laughter]

Q : The more you find the more you get...

U.G.: If you try to destroy the authority of others, you in your own way become the authority for others. How to avoid that [becoming an authority] is really a problem for me. But in some sense it's not really a problem.

Q : But you should accept them [seekers].

U.G.: No. I cannot because it is very clear to me that I cannot be of any help to them, and that they don't need any help from me. What they are interested in they can get somewhere else. There are so many people who are selling in the market-place. They are interested in selling comforters. That is where these people should go, and not hang around me.

Q : Can you say something about discipline? For example, Japan is founded on discipline.

U.G.: True. The whole thought of religious thought is built on the foundation of discipline. Discipline to me means a sort of masochism. We are all masochists. We torture ourselves because we think that suffering is a means to achieve our spiritual goals. That's unfortunate.

Q : Is life difficult?

U.G.: Life is difficult. So discipline sounds very attractive to people. With great honour we say, "He has suffered a lot". We admire those who have suffered a lot to achieve their goals. As a matter of fact, the whole religious thinking is built on the foundation of suffering.

Q : We have got all this at the cross.

U.G.: At the cross. If not for religion, you suffer for the cause of your country in the name of patriotism...

Q : For your town, for your family...

U.G.: Those who impose that kind of discipline on us are sadists. But unfortunately we are all being masochists in accepting that. We torture ourselves in the hope of achieving something...we are slaves of our ideas and beliefs. We are not ready to throw them out. If we succeed in throwing them out, we replace them with another set of beliefs, another body of discipline. Those who are marching into the battlefield and are ready to be killed today in the name of democracy, in the name of freedom, in the name of communism, are no different from those who threw themselves to the lions in the arenas. The Romans watched that fun with great joy. How are we different from them? Not a bit. We love it. To kill and to be killed is the foundation of our culture.

The Build-up Of Sex And Love

Q : Human relationships have become a kind of commercial exchange - in the sense of, "If you give me something, I will give you something". Could we go into that a bit?

U.G.: Yes. That's a fact. We do not want to accept it because it destroys the myth that human relationships are something marvellous and extraordinary. We are not honest, decorous and decent enough to admit that all relationships are built on the foundation of, "What I get out of this relationship?" It is nothing but mutual gratific ation. If that is absent, no relationship is possible. You keep the relationship going for social reasons, or for reasons of children, property, and security. All this is part and parcel of the relationship business. But when it fails and does not give us what we really want, we superimpose on it what we call "love". So it is just not possible to have any relationship on any basis except on the level of mutual gratification.

The whole culture has created, for its own reasons, this situation for us through its value system. The value system demands that relationship be based on love. But the most important element is security and then possessiveness. You want to possess the other individual. When your hold on the other becomes weaker for various reasons, your relationship wears out. You cannot maintain this "lovy-dovey" relationship all the time.

The relationship between a man and a woman is based on the images that the two create for themselves of each other. So, the actual relationship between the two individuals is a relationship between the two images. But your image keeps changing, and so does the other person's. To keep the image constant is just not possible. So, when everything else fails, we use this final, last card in the pack, "love", with all the marvellous and romantic ideations around it.

To me, love implies two [persons]. Wherever there is a division, whether it is within you or without you, there is conflict. That relationship cannot last long. As far as I am concerned, relationships are formed and then they are dissolved immediately. Both these things happen in the same frame, if I may use that word. That is really the problem. You may think that I am a very crude man, but if anybody talks to me about love, to me it is a 'four-letter word'. That is the only basic relationship between man and woman. But it is a social problem for us as to what kind of a relationship you should have. Even in the days of my youth it was not possible amongst the Brahmins to marry unless the couple belonged to the same sub-caste. It was worse than the racial stuff in other countries. They had a strange idea of maintaining family traditions. What is tradition after all? It is unwillingness to change with the changing time. We change a little when we are forced to by conditions. But the fact is that change is not in the interests of the mechanism of our thinking.

Unfortunately, we have blown this business of sex out of proportion. It is just a simple biological need of the living organism. The body is interested in only two things - to survive, and to reproduce one like itself. It is not interested in anything else. But sex has become a tremendous problem for us, because we turned the basic biological functioning of the body into a pleasure movement. You see, if there is no thought, there is no sex at all.

The second problem is that it is not just the sex act that is important [to us], but the build-up that is there, the romantic structure that we have built around the love play. If you look at a beautiful woman, for example, the moment you say that it is a woman; you have already created a problem – "A beautiful woman"! Then it is more pleasurable to hold her hands than just to look at her. It is more pleasurable to embrace her, even more pleasurable to kiss her, and so on. It is the build-up that is really the problem. The moment you say that she is a beautiful woman; culture comes into the picture.

Here [pointing to himself] the build-up is totally absent because there is no way that these [pointing to his eyes] can be focused on any particular object continuously. For all you know, when that beautiful woman opens her mouth, she might have the ugliest teeth that a woman could have. So, you see, that [the eyes] has moved from there to here and again from here to something else, as perhaps, to her movements. It is [the eyes are] constantly changing its focus and there is no way that you can maintain this build-up. What is there is only the physical attraction. You can never be free from that. All those people - these saints - are tortured with the idea of controlling that natural attraction. But that natural attraction is something that should not be condemned. You don't tell yourself that you are a godman, a realized man, an enlightened man or a saint, and that you should not think these thoughts. That [telling yourself] is really the problem. They are not honest enough to admit that. So whenever a saint comes to me, or one who practices celibacy, I am very ruthless with him. I ask him, "Do you really mean to say that you never have wet dreams?" I tell him, "To practice celibacy in the name of your spiritual pursuit is a crime against nature". If the man is impotent or if for some reason the woman happens to be barren, then it is a different story. Why the religious thinking of man has emphasized denial of sex, as a means to his spiritual attainment is something that I cannot understand. Maybe because that is the way you can control people. Sex is the most powerful drive.

Q : So sex is a natural thing and it is not dirty.

U.G.: Right. Sex is a very natural thing. You see, if you don't have sex, the semen probably goes out through your urine or in some other way. After all, the sex glands have to function. If they don't function normally, you are an abnormal individual. But we are not ready to accept these facts, because it undermines the very foundation of human culture. We cannot accept the fact that we are just biological beings and nothing more. It is something like saying that in the field of economics you are not controlled by the laws of supply and demand. But actually, in the field of economics you are. Likewise, in the political field the laws of politics control us. But we are not ready to accept the basic, fundamental fact that we are just biological beings, and all that is happening within the body is a result of hormonal activity. It is pure and simple chemistry. If there is any problem there [in the body], it is too presumptuous on my part to tell you, as you are a sex therapist. Problems in that area cannot be solved in any other way than by trying to change the chemistry of the whole body. I think our whole thinking has to be put on a different track. I don't know; I am just suggesting. I may be wrong. I am not competent enough.

Q : What track would that be?

U.G.: It is all chemical. If, as they say, desires are hormones, then the whole ethical code and culture that we have created through centuries to control the behaviour of human beings are false. So, desire cannot be false. Anything that is happening within the [human] organism cannot be false.

Q : Are you saying that there will always be sexual desire even without thought?

U.G.: There is no sex at all without thought. Thought is memory. These experts make fun of me when I say that the most important of all glands is the thymus gland. When I discussed this subject with some physiologists and doctors they made fun on me. Naturally so, because according to them, the gland is inactive. If it is activated through any external means, it would be an abnormal situation. But, you know, the thymus is the most important gland, and feelings operate there without the element of thought.

Q : From the thymus...

U.G.: Yes, from the thymus. You see, medical technology

has ignored that for a very long time. They considered any unusual condition of the gland to be an abnormality and tried to treat it. It is true that when you reach the adolescent age, it becomes inactive, and then your feelings are controlled by your ideas.

Q : By culture rather than by natural biology...

U.G.: Than by natural biology. Feeling, to me, is like this: if you trip, I don't actually trip along with you; but the whole of my being is involved in that 'tripping over'. That is the kind of feeling that I am talking about; all other feelings are emotions and thoughts. The distinction between feeling [not in the sense that I mentioned just now] and thought is not really something...

Q : It is just artificial.

U.G.: It is very artificial. It is cultural. "The heart is more important than the head" and all such nonsense are absolute poppycock. When once this [U.G.'s] kind of disturbance takes place in the hormonal balance of the human body through this catastrophe, through this calamity, through whatever you want to call it, not only is the thymus activated but all other glands such as the pineal and the pituitary are also activated. People ask me, "Why don't you submit yourself to medical testing to validate all these claims?" I tell them that I am not selling these claims.

What I have against medical technology is that you want to understand the functioning of these things with a motive. When once you have some idea of how these glands function, how the activation of these things will help mankind, you are not going to use it for the benefit of mankind.

Q : And that is the reason why you are not interested in ...

U.G.: Not interested in studying all that. If you don't accept what I am saying, it is just fine with me. If some top physician wants to reject what I say, that fellow will say that I am talking rubbish. Bu t now volumes have been written in America on the subject of the thymus gland. I am not claiming any special knowledge of these things. What I am trying to say is that the feelings felt at the thymus are quite different from the feeling induced by thoughts.

Sex has to be put in its proper place as one of the natural functionings of the body. It is solely, mainly and wholly for the purpose of reproducing or procreating something like this [the body]. It has no other place in the functioning of the body.

Q : If one is only interested in procreating, then one wouldn't find any other function for sexuality?

U.G.: There is no way you can go back now, because thought always interferes with sex. It has become a pleasure movement. I am not saying anything against it. I go to the extent of telling people that if it is possible for you to have sex with your mother without any problem, psychological or spiritual, than that will put an end to your sex. You see, the whole thing is built on your ideas. I am not advocating incest as a way of life. For this [the body] there is no such thing as incest at all. It is the guilt problem, the psychological problem, the religious problem, which says that it has to be this way and not that way. If it is possible for a human being to have sex without a second thought, without any regret, with his sister, daughter, or mother, then this [sex] is finished once and for all. It falls into its proper place. I am not suggesting it as a therapy. Please don't get me wrong.

Q : No, no...

U.G.: What I am trying to say is that it is just not possible to have sex with your wife or with anybody without the build-up.

Q : So sex goes after that...

U.G.: Sex goes after that. Thereafter, what you are left with is the natural functioning of the sex glands. If they are not used, the semen will go out through urine. All these claims of the spiritual teachers that it will move from the *muladhara* to the *sahasrara* are rubbish. Don't believe all that nonsense. If the semen is not used, it goes out through your urine whether you are a saint or a godman or a sinner. You may or may not have wet dreams, but still it goes out.

Q : The body still goes on functioning?

U.G.: Yes. There seems to be an abnormal functioning here [with U.G.]. What you call estrogen in the case of, what is that, I am not familiar with all these terms...

Q : Well, the female hormones.

U.G.: The female hormones. You see, as they say, for the first few days or weeks, the sex of an embryo is not differentiated, but somewhere along the line, it is decided by...

Q : One becomes male...

U.G.: One becomes male. Here [in U.G.] the body goes back into that stage where it is neither male nor female. It is not the androgynous thing that they talk about.

Q : More psychological...

U.G.: It is more psychological. So, we have to revise all our ideas about this whole business of sex. We give a tremendous importance to sex, and so the denial of it becomes such an obsession with people. In India they even moved away from that denial and created what is called Tantric sex. It was the highest pleasure that human beings could have. Sex through Tantra was considered the highest. That was the reason why they created in Brazil, and probably in some other countries too, the coupling of the male and the female organs. We have in India all that nonsense – the temples, and then a temple for the bull, a symbol of virility. All these were admired and worshiped. This is the other extreme [to denial of sex]: indulgence in sex became a spiritual pursuit. They talked of achieving spiritual goals, enlightenment, or what have you, through sex, and called it Tantric sex. Whether it is ordinary sex or Tantric sex, or you go and have sex with a prostitute, it's all the same.

Q : But I can understand why people would be interested in sex as a means to attain the so-called spirituality. Because at the moment of intense sexual involvement, or orgasm, people have the feeling that they are not there any more...

U.G.: That feeling is temporary, very temporary.

Q : It is just for a flash of a second.

U.G.: Not even a flash of a second. Even there, the division cannot be absent. Even in extreme grief you get the feeling that you are not there. What happens if the body goes through unbearable pain? You become unconscious. It is then that the body has a chance of taking care of that pain. If it cannot, then you go.

Q : You mean to say that at the moment of orgasm, which is just a flash of a second, the person *is* there?

U.G.: The fact is that the person is very much there even at the moment when there is peak sex experience. The experience has already been captured by your memory. Otherwise you have no way of experiencing that as a peak moment. If that peak moment remained as a peak moment; that would be just the end of sex; that would be the end of everything.

Q : You remember there was a peak moment, but you cannot remember the actual feeling?

U.G.: That is not important. The fact that you remember it as a peak moment and want to repeat it over and over again implies that it has already become part of your experiencing structure. You want it always and then want to extend it for longer and longer periods of time. This is one of the most idiotic things to do. I read somewhere that a long time ago they tortured a woman to have a continuous orgasm for half-an-hour or one hour, I don't know. But why put her through that torture? What for? What do you prove by that? It is also a fad for people here in the West. They want to make it last longer. It is just for a fraction of a second, whether it is in the female or in the male. You are a therapist. You probably know a lot more than I do. But I think that there is really no justification for extending the orgasm longer that its natural duration. It has become an obsession with some people, and if they don't have it, their sex act seems very futile.

Q : It becomes an addiction as well?

U.G.: Like any other addiction. All these things I observed myself. I did not learn about from anyone. I saw them happen in my own life. I told my wife about them. Every time my wife talked of love I asked her what all that nonsense was about. The only basis of our relationship was sex.

I denied myself sex for twenty-five years pursuing spiritual goals. Then I suddenly realized, "Look, this is ridiculous. Celibacy has nothing to do with it. I have wet dreams. Sex is burning inside me. Why the hell am I denying myself sex? Why the hell am I torturing myself?" I asked my teacher, "Are you sure you didn't have wet dreams any time?" He blushed. He did not have the courage to give me an answer.

Q : Could you tell me whether you had them?

U.G.: Oh, yes. That did not mean that I moved to the other extreme and practiced promiscuity as my way of life. The most beautiful girls from Holland, America, and everywhere surrounded me. I didn't even have to ask for it. But then, I felt that this was not the way to understand the problem of sex. The relationship with my wife was the only relationship I had then. She understood my attitude toward sex, but she still had some [of her own] ideas of love. She always asked me, "You are surrounded by the most beautiful woman here. You are a very handsome man by any definition. Why don't you have sex with them? Do you have a problem of guilt or loyalty?" I told her, "Actually, if there is an act of infidelity on my part, the whole thing will change". I warned her, "Don't talk of all this nonsense. As a conversation piece, it's fine". It is not that there was a moral or ethical problem. I wanted to find out about sex, and I realized that I was actually using her for my pleasure.

Q : And you could be frank about that?

U.G.: Yes, we always discussed it.

Q : There was no love involved?

U.G.: No. Yet she was the finest woman I could have been married to.

Q : So you said, "I am just interested in sex"?

U.G.: She also realized that that was all. But the only problem that we had was concerning children. She wanted more children because of her genes. My wife was the twenty-first pregnancy of her mother.

Q : Twenty-first?

U.G.: Yes. And so, wanting more children was a genetic problem. That was the real problem between us. We even went to see Marie Stopes in London. You may have heard of her.

Q : To sort it out...?

U.G.: To find out. My wife was also against birth control and such other measures. She tried to sort these things out. She was telling me that by nursing a child for a longer time, pregnancy could be delayed. All kinds of strange ideas! She was not ready to go to a doctor and finish it with an abortion. But somewhere along the line she did have an abortion, as we did not want to have more children.

Apart from all this, I did have a one-night stand. It was not with a cheap call girl or a prostitute. It was with one of the richest women around. And that finished the whole thing. There was no more sex after that. You will be surprised at that.

Q : That was when you were still having a relationship with your wife?

U.G.: Yes.

Q : The affair finished it all!

U.G. : It just happened to me. I happened to be in this woman's place. I don't want to go into all the sordid details. That was thirty-three years ago. It was finished! That was the end of sex for me. I felt that I was using that woman for my own pleasure. It was not an ethical problem. The fact that I used that woman hit me very hard. I said to myself, "She may be a willing victim, a willing partner in this whole game, but I cannot do this any more". That was the end of it, and it created a problem for my wife also, not in the sense that she revolted against me but in the sense that I denied sex to her too.

Q : She felt rejected?

U.G.: Yes. She felt guilty for pushing me to that extent. It is not that she actually did that. She did not push me into that situation. Anyway, the incident finished sex for me. But that did not finish the sex urge *per se*, because just as in women there is a natural rhythm in men. I could notice that there was a peak sometimes, and for months and months you didn't even know about it.

Q : It is so with a woman as well.

U.G.: Yes, just like there is period for women. It is impossible for a woman and a man to attain orgasm at the same time. We are programmed differently.

Q : It cannot be synchronized.

U.G.: If that could be synchronized, it would be a marvellous thing. But there is no way you can do that at all. So, until this [the natural state that U.G. stumbled into] happened to me, the powerful drive [sex] was still there. But it knew that the semen would go through the urine or some other way. That didn't bother me because I was determined to figure out and solve this problem [of sex] for myself and by myself. I did not go to a therapist. I never believed in any therapy. So it resolved on its own and·by itself. Sex has a place in the organism. It is a very simple functioning of the body. Its interest is only to create. I discovered these things by myself.

I will give you another example. We were about to make love, and my two-year-old girl cried. We had to break up, and you can't imagine what violent feelings I had that time. I just wanted to strangle that child! Of course, I did not act on those feelings. I could have. That was the frame of my mind. I said to myself, "That is the blood of my own blood, to use an idiotic phrase, bone of my bone - my own child. How can I have such thoughts? There is something wrong here [pointing to himself]." I told myself, "You are not a spiritual man, you are not what you think you are and what people think you are." I was lecturing on the Theosophical platforms everywhere. I said to myself, "You are 'this', and 'this' is you. This is what you are - all this violence".

Q : Is sex violence?

U.G.: Sex is violence. But it is a necessary violence for this body. It's a pain.

Q : As far as procreation is concerned...

U.G.: All creative things are painful. The birth of a child is a very natural thing. But to call it a traumatic experience and build up a tremendous structure of theories around it is something I am not concerned with. It cannot be a traumatic experience. That is why, after all this violence you go to sleep. You feel tried. That is how nature functions. All creations in nature are like that. I don't call it pain or violence. Volcanic eruptions, earthquakes, storms, and overflowing rivers are all part of nature. You cannot say that there is only chaos or that there is only order. Chaos and order happen almost at the same time. Birth and death are simultaneous processes.

I am not against promiscuity, nor am I against celibacy. But I want to emphasize one basic thing, that is, in the pursuit of your spiritual matters it doesn't really make any difference whether you practice celibacy or indulge in sex and call it Tantric sex. It is comforting to believe that you are having Tantric sex and not sex with a call girl or a prostitute. To say that there is more 'feeling' or more closeness when you have sex for spiritual reasons is absolute gibberish.

Q : So there is nothing to Tantric sex?

U.G.: There are so many people who are doing this kind of thing in the name of enlightenment. That is detestable to me. They are not honest enough to admit that they are using that [the lure of enlightenment] for fulfilling their lust. That is why they are running these brothels. These kinds of gurus are pimps.

Q : Rajneesh became famous for that...

U.G.: Yes, someone asked me, "What do you have to say about him after his death?" I said that the world has never seen such a pimp nor will it ever see one in the future. [Laughs]

Q : He was very good. I mean very professional.

U.G.: Yes, professional. He combined Western therapies, the Tantric system, and everything that you could find in the books. He made a big business out of it. He took money from the boys; he took money from girls, and kept it for himself. He is dead and so we don't say anything. *Nil nisi bonum* (Of the dead speak not unless it be good) [Laughter].

Q : But if we can go back to...

U.G.: What I want to say is that unfortunately, society, culture, or whatever you want to call it, has separated the sex activity and put it on a different level, instead of treating it as a simple functioning of the living organism. It is a basic thing in nature. Survival and reproduction are basic things in the living organisms.

Q : And the rest is an artificial build-up...

U.G.: You can change the areas, you can change the ideas, and you can write books. It really doesn't matter. As far as I am concerned, I don't tell anybody what he or she should or should not do. My interest is to point out that this is the situation and say, "Take it or leave it".

Q : Without the build up, without the culture, without thought, there would still be a sexual functioning of the body, but there wouldn't be anyone to make a problem out of it?

U.G.: No, look. Anything we touch we turn into a problem; and sex even more so, because this is the most powerful drive there. If you translate it [into pleasure] and push it into an area where it does not really belong, namely, the pleasure movement, we will then create problems. When once you create a problem, the demand to deal with that problem within that framework is bound to arise. So, that is where you come in [with sex therapy etc.]. I have nothing against sex therapists, but the problem [sex as pleasure] has to be solved by people. Otherwise they become neurotic. They don't know what to do with themselves. Not only that, but everything, God, truth, reality, liberation, *moksha*, is ultimate pleasure. We are not ready to accept that.

Q : But sex is very concrete?

U.G.: Very concrete. It is tangible. That is why it has become a very powerful factor in our lives. That is why there is also a demand to put limitations on it by culture, first in the name of religion, and then in the name of the family, law, war, and a hundred other things. This [the demand to limit sex] is nothing but the outgrowth of the religious thinking of man. What's the difference?

Q : In spite of all these laws they just cannot do anything. It just goes on and on...

U.G.: It goes on. You talk of the sacredness of life and condemn abortion. This is the same old idiotic Christian idea persisting, which turned every woman into a criminal. And then you go on and kill hundreds and thousands of people in the name of your flag, in the name of patriotism. That is the way things are. Not that it is in your interest to change it, but change is something, which this structure [i.e., thought] is not interested in. It only talks of change. But you know things are changing constantly.

Q : This artificial build-up of sexual excitement is actually damaging the body, but there are a lot of people who think that, because tension is released and you feel more relaxed, it is good for health.

U.G.: You first create a tension. All this fantasy, all this romantic nonsense, is building up tension. When once the tension is built, it has to dissolve itself. That is why rest becomes essential and you go to sleep. You fall asleep because you are tired and exhausted. ...The aftereffects are bound to follow. That's fine, but it's wearing you out in the long run.

Q : Could you comment on the difference in sexual behaviour between men and women that is sweeping the West now a days?

U.G.: [Laughs] You mean the feminist movement? It's a joke.

Q : In my work I am also concerned with sexual violence such as men having sex with women or children against their will, and all the damage that they do to children. You hardly see that sort of physical sexual violence in women and children. Why is it that a lot of men use children and women as the object of sexual violence?

U.G.: That, you see, is a sociological problem. I think you probably know much on this subject. I don't know. I can't say much about that problem. But it's really unfortunate that man got away with everything for centuries while society ignored women. Half the population of this planet was neglected, humiliated and treated as doormats. Even the Bible tells you that the woman is made out of the rib of man. What preposterous nonsense! You see, women's intelligence is lost for this culture. Not only here, it's the same everywhere.

Q: So, where does this [violence] arise from? From time immemorial?

U.G.: The other party is also responsible for that. You are praising the woman as a darling and she accepts that minor role. The woman is also to be blamed for it. I am not overly enthusiastic about all these feminist movements today. It is a revolt that really has no basis; it's more of a reaction.

Q: You mean both parties are responsible for the situation?

U.G.: Both are responsible for this. I say this very often. One of the leaders of the feminist movement visited me and asked, "What do you have to say of our movement?" I said, "I am on your side, but you have to realize one very fundamental thing. As long as, you depend on man for your sexual needs, so long you are not a free person. If you use a vibrator for your sexual satisfaction, that is a different matter." "You are very crude," she said. I am not crude. What I am saying is a fact. As long as you depend up on something or somebody there is scope for exploitation. I am not against the feminist movement. They ought to have every right. Even today, in the same job a woman is paid less in the United States than a man. Why?

Q : That is culture, of course.

U.G.: There was a time when I believed that if women were to rule this world, it would be a different story. We had a woman prime minister in India and a woman prime minister in Sri Lanka. There was a lady prime minister in England. I don't know whether that will happen in America and whether a woman will be the president of the United States. But I tell you they [women] are as ruthless as any others. In fact, more ruthless. So this dream of mine was shattered [Laughs] when I saw that woman there in Jerusalem, what was her name...

Q : Golda Meir...

U.G.: So, it is not a question of a man running the show or a woman running the show, but it is the system that corrupts.

Q : There wouldn't be any inherent difference between man and woman in this tendency to dominate anywhere and at any time.

U.G.: Power games are part of culture.

Q : There is no biology involved?

U.G.: Now they are talking of hormones. I really don't know. They say it is the hormones that are responsible for the violence. If that is so, what do we do?

Q : We need a woman still...

U.G.: Assuming for a moment that the advantage that we [men] have had for centuries is not a culturally instigated thing, but a hormonal phenomenon, you have to deal with it in a different way and not put that person on the couch, analyze him, and say that his mother or great-grandmother was responsible for his aggression. That is too absurd and silly. So, we have to find some way. The basic question that we have to ask ourselves is: what kind of a human being do you want? But unfortunately we have placed before ourselves the model of a perfect being. The perfect being is a godman or a spiritual man or an *avatar*, or some such being. But forcing everyone to fit into that mould is the cause of our tragedy. It is just not possible for us all to be like that.

Q : But it is so tempting to be like that.

U.G.: Once upon a time, the sceptre and the crown, the church, and the pontiffs, were all worshiped. Later the kings revolted against that, and then the royal family came to be admired and worshiped. Where are they now? Others have eliminated royalty and have created the office of the president. We are told that you should not insult the head of the state. Until yesterday, he was your neighbour, and now he becomes the president of your republic. Why do you have to worship a king or a president? The whole hierarchical structure, whether of the past or of the present, is exactly the same.

Q : But there seems to be a need in a person to seek for something which he thinks is higher that himself.

U.G.: That something is what we would like to be. That is why we admire and worship someone. The whole hierarchical structure is built on that foundation. It is all right with the politicians, let alone the monarchy and the church. Even the top tennis player – or a movie star – is a hero. They are models for us. And the culture is responsible for this situation. It is not only the physiological differences, the hormonal differences, if there are any, (I don't know and wouldn't know), but the whole commercialism has that effect. You walk into any store or watch any commercial on the television; they [the ad men] are always telling you how you should dress, and how you should beautify yourself. The beauty of a woman depends upon the ideas of Helena Rubenstein or Elizabeth Arden, or someone else. Now half the stores here contain cosmetics for men. I am not condemning it, but pointing out that that is the way of our life. So the ad man is telling you what kind of clothes you should wear, and what colours should match what other colours. He is telling you this all the time. So, you are influenced by what he is telling you. And you want what he wants you to want. How are we going to deal with this problem? I don't know. It is not for me to answer. It is for those people who want to deal with these problems.

Q: You are in a different state, and maybe normal human beings...

U.G.: Who is normal? The normal person is a statistical concept. But how can this [whatever U.G.] be a model? This [whatever has happened to U.G] has no value in the sense that whatever I am cannot be fitted into any value system. It is of no use for the world. It has no value for me and it has no value for the world. You may very well ask me the question, "Why the hell are we talking about all this?" Because you had some questions to throw at me, and what I am doing is to put them in a proper perspective. I only say, "Look at it this way".

I am not interested in winning you over to my point of view, because I have no point of view. And there is no way you can win me over to your point of view. It is not that I am dogmatic or any such thing. It is impossible for you to win me over to your point of view. During a conversation like this, somebody throws words at me like, "Oh, you are very this or very that". It is also a point of view. So how do you think these two points of view can be reconciled, and for what purpose do you want to reconcile them? You feel good because you have won him to your point of view. You use your logic and your rationality because you are more intelligent than I am. All this is nothing but a power play.

You feel good, like the people who claim to render service to mankind. That is the "do-gooder's high". You help an old woman across the street and you feel it is good. But it is a self-centered activity. You are interested only in some brownie points, but you shamelessly tell others that you are doing a social turn. I am not cynical. I am just pointing out that it [this feeling] is a do-gooder's high. It is just like any other high. If I admit this, living becomes very simple. If you admit this, then it also shows what a detestable creature you are. You are doing it for yourself, and you tell others and yourself that you are doing it for the benefit of others. I am not cynical. You may say that I am a cynic, but cynicism is realism. The cynic's feet are firmly fixed on the ground.

Q : But I don't find this cynical at all. It makes perfect sense to me. I would like to come back to this moral seeking that we are doing constantly and in every field, including the so-called spiritual field...

U.G.: Politics, economics, you name it...

Q : Is it not different in the spiritual field?

U.G.: Why is it different? It is exactly the same. We found ourselves in a situation where only spirituality mattered. And now there are movie stars instead of Jesus. So many people have movie stars, tennis players, or wrestlers as their models, depending upon what their particular fancy is.

Q : And they like it. But to you it is a different story.

U.G.: I visited a friend of mine. He was condemning his daughters for having the pictures of movie stars in the bathrooms. But when we walked into his living room, he had my photo on his table. I asked him, "What's the difference between the two?"

Q : It's the same thing.

U.G.: One day many Rajneesh disciples visited me in Mumbai. My host happened to be one of the top movie directors. He was very close to Rajneesh. He spent years and years practicing all the techniques taught by Rajneesh. But after he met me he walked out on him. And in his living room, there used to be a massive picture of Rajneesh. After his encounter with me he removed it and put it in the cupboard and then put my picture there. Look what he has done!

Q : Exchange one for the other.

U.G.: Yes. Just like divorce in America. You divorce one woman and then the new wife comes. You put the old wife's picture and your children's pictures all in the attic and replace them with the pictures of the new wife's parents, grandparents and children. [Laughter]

Q : Do you care about that?

U.G.: No, no. I just pointed out the absurdity of it. That is all that they can do – replace one illusion with another illusion, one belief with another belief. But if the belief comes to an end, that's the end of everything.

Q : But you explained that there is nothing that one can do to change this.

U.G.: Not a thing. If you are lucky enough [I don't know, 'lucky enough' may not be the appropriate phrase], to find yourself where there is no attempt on your part to get out of the trap, then it may be a different story. But the fact of the matter is that the more you try to get out of the trap, the more deeply you are entrenched in it. This is very difficult to understand.

Q : That's the trap - wanting to get out of it.

U.G.: Yes. I tell all those who want to discuss with me the question of how to decondition yourself, how to live with an unconditioned mind, that the very thing that they are doing is conditioning them, conditioning them in a different way. You are just picking up a new lingo instead of using the usual one. You begin to use the new lingo and feel good. That's all. But this is conditioning you in exactly the same way; that's all it can do. The physical body [U.G. is now referring to himself] is conditioning in such a way that it acts as intelligence. Conditioning is intelligence here. There is no need for you to think.

Q : But there is no conditioning of the body.

U.G.: The conditioning of the body is its intelligence. That is the native intelligence of the body. I am not talking about the instinct. The intelligence of the body is necessary for its survival. That intelligence is quite different from the intellect that we have developed. Our intellect is no match for that intelligence. If you don't think, the body can take care of itself in a situation where it finds itself in danger. Whenever the body is faced with danger, it relies upon itself and not your thinking or your intellect. If, on the other hand, you just think, then you are frightened. The fear makes it difficult for you to act. People ask me, "How come you take walks with the cobras?" I have never done it with a tiger or any other wild animal. But I don't think I would be frightened of them either. If there is no fear in you, then you can take walks with them. The fear emits certain odours, which the cobra senses. The cobra senses that you are a dangerous thing. Naturally, the cobra has to take the first step. Otherwise, it is one of the most beautiful creatures that nature has created. They are the most lovable creatures. You can take a walk with them and you can talk to them.

Q : Do they talk back?

U.G.: It is like a one-way seminar. [Laughter] I don't know. Once a friend of mine, a movie star, visited me in an ashram that I was staying in. She asked me whether it was all an exaggeration that cobras visited me and that I took walks with them. I said, "You wait till the evening or night, and you will be surprised". Later, when we went for a walk at dusk, not just one cobra, but its wife, children, and grandchildren - about fifteen of them, appeared out of nowhere.

Q : The whole family?

U.G.: The whole family. My guest ran away. If you try to play with it [with the idea of taking walks with cobras], you are in trouble. It is your fear that is responsible for the situation you find yourself in. It is your fear that creates a problem for the cobra; then it has to take the first step.

If the cobra kills you, you are only one person. Whereas we kill hundreds and thousands of cobras for no reason. If you destroy these cobras, then the field mice will have a field day, and you will find that they destroy the crops. There is a tremendous balance in nature. Our indiscretions are responsible for the imbalance in nature.

If I find a cobra trying to harm a child or somebody, I would tell him (I may not kill the cobra, you see) or tell the cobra to go away. (Laughter) You know, the cobra will go away. But you, on the other hand, have to kill. Why do you have to kill hundreds and thousands for no reason? The fear that they will harm us in the future is what is responsible for such acts. But we are creating an imbalance in nature; and then you will have to kill the field mice also. You feed the cats with vitamins or a special kind of a food, and if the cat tries to kill a field mouse, sometimes you want to save the mouse. What for? Even cats do not eat mice any more, because they are used to the food from the supermarkets. But the cats still play with mice and kill them for no reason. They leave them uneaten in the fields. It's amazing. I noticed it several times.

Q : They are corrupted cats?

U.G.: Corrupted cats. By associating themselves with us, even cats and rats become like human beings. You also give identity to the cats and names to the dogs. Human culture has spoiled those animals. Unfortunately, we spoil the animals by making them our pets.

Q : Are you tired? Would you like to stop?

U.G.: No. It's up to you. This is your property, not mine. I have nothing to do with what I have said. It is you who have brought this out from me. What you do with it is your affair. You have the copyright over whatever has come out. I don't sit here and think about these things at all. At no time do I do that.

Q : It doesn't concern you at all?

U.G.: No. It doesn't concern me at all. You come here and throw all these things at me. I am not actually giving you any answers. I am only trying to focus or spotlight the whole thing and say, "This is the way you look at these things; but look at them this [other] way. Then you will be able to find out the solutions for yourself without anyone's help". That is all. My interest is to point out to you that you can walk, and please throw away all those crutches. If you were really handicapped, I wouldn't advise you to do any such thing. But you are made to feel by other people that you are handicapped so that they could sell you those crutches. Throw them away and you can walk. That's all that I can say. "If I fall....", that is your fear. Put the crutches away, and you are not going to fall.

Q : Is the handicap just a belief?

U.G.: When we are made to believe that we are handicapped, we become dependent on the crutches. The modern gurus supply you with mechanized crutches.

Q : Why do we feel that we are handicapped, why this conflict, this turmoil?

U.G.: The whole thing is put in there by culture.

Q : But it is there!

U.G.: Where? Where is it?

Q : Somewhere I can sense it and feel it, and I feel bothered by it.

U.G.: But you are giving life to it through constantly thinking about these things. You have a tremendous investment in all these things. But these are all memories, ideas.

Q : What is memory?

U.G.: I don't really know what memory is. We were told that, "To recall a specific thing at a specific time" is memory. We repeated this definition as students of psychology. But it is much more that that. They say that memory is in the neurons. If it is all in the neurons, where is it located in them? The brain does not seem to be the centre of memory. Cells seem to have their own memory. So, where is that memory? Is it transmitted through genes? I really don't know. Some of these questions have no answers so far. Probably one of these days they will find out.

I believe that the problems of this planet can be solved through the help of the tremendous high-tech and technology at our disposal. But the benefits that we have accrued through these advancements have not yet percolated to the level of all the people living on this planet. Technology has benefited only a microscopic number of people. It seems that even without the help of high-tech and technology it is possible for us to feed twelve billion people. When nature has provided us with such bounty, why is it that three-fourths of the people are underfed? Why are they all starving? They are starving because we are responsible for their problems. That is the problem that is facing us all today.

Even in Iraq it's the same. The game that is going on there is only to dominate and control the resources of the world. That is the naked truth and the rest of it is absolute rubbish. Whether you kill an Iraqi or an American it really doesn't matter. The president of the United States says, "I am ready to sacrifice Americans". For what? When the coffins start arriving in America, they will sing a different song. But that is not the point. I am not on this side or that. The reality of the situation *is* that.

The other problem is: how do we change a human being, and for what purpose? If the purpose is to correct physical deformities, we are lucky that medical technology will help us. If a child has some kind of handicap, there is something that can be done to change it. So, people have to be thankful to medical technology. Nature is not concerned about the handicap one way or another. One more person added to the population. So, if any changes are necessary in human beings, and if you want them to function differently by freeing them from all the things that the ethical, cultural, legal structure is failing to free them from and thereby create a different kind of people, then probably only genetic engineering could come to our aid. Codes of ethics, morals, and the legal structure are not going to help. They have not helped so far. They have not achieved anything. But through the help of genetic engineering we may be able to free the individuals from the thieving tendencies, from violence, greed, and jealousy. But the question is, for what? I don't know for what?

Q : What the genetic engineers are doing will only give them more power!

U.G.: The engineers are helped by the state. They are the victims of the state. They are doing this not, as they claim, for humanitarian reasons or altruistic purposes, but for recognition, for a Nobel Prize, or for some prestigious awards.

Q : So, if they find a solution, then...?

U.G.: They will hand it over to the state, and it will become easier for the leaders to send people like robots to the battlefields and to kill without question. That is inevitable. So what is it that we are actually doing? As I see it – and this is my doomsday song - there is nothing that you can do to reverse this whole trend. Individually probably, you can jump off the tiger. But no matter what you say to that man who is frightened of jumping off and is continuing the tiger ride, it is not going to help him. Actually, you don't even have to jump off; [Laughs] you can continue to ride. There is no problem there. You are not in conflict with the society because the world cannot be any different. If someone wants to be on the top, if it is part of his power game, then he talks of changing the world; he talks of creating heaven or paradise on earth. But I want to know when.

During the Second World War we were all made to believe that it was a war to end all wars. What nonsense they talked! Has it ended wars? Wars have been going on and on. We were made to believe that the First World War was waged to make the world safe for democracy. [Laughs] Oh boy! We are all made to believe all kinds of stuff. If you believe your leader, or if you believe what the newspaperman is telling you, you will believe anybody and anything.

Q : But even realizing this doesn't change anything?

U.G.: Changes... Why are you concerned about the world and the other man?

Q : But you know, Sir, when you realize that you are on the wrong side of the tiger...

U.G.: You have not realized anything. If there is really that realization there is an action. I don't like to use the phrase "freed from all that", but you are not in conflict any more. There is no way you can bring the conflict [to an end]. The conflict is there because of the neurotic situation that the culture has put in you.

Q : And in realizing that...

U.G.: How do you realize? The instrument that you have at your disposal…

Q : My intellect...

U.G.: That intellect is the one that is responsible for the neurotic situation. This is the human situation. There is no way you can resolve your problems through that instrument. But we are not ready to accept that it can only create problems and cannot help us to solve them.

Q : But even if you accept that, would it make a difference?

U.G.: No.

Q : This is so clear...

U.G.: No. It is not a fact there. To me, it is a fact. "It is so," means there is no further movement there to do anything about it. That is the end of the whole thing.

Q : If it is so...

U.G.: It cannot be so for you. If it is so; that is the end of your dialogue. You are on your own.

Q : I can see that.

U.G.: You are on your own. You will not talk about me. If you talk about me it is just another story you are telling, picked up somewhere else. So what will come out of it is anybody's guess. What you will say will not be the same.

Q : I don't catch that...

U.G.: If you are lucky enough to throw the whole thing out of your system, the whole of what everyone thought, felt and experienced...

Q : Can we?

U.G.: You cannot, and there is nothing that you can do about it. You don't even complete that sentence. The situation is such that you don't even tell yourself that there is nothing that you can do about it.

Q : So when I say to myself that I can do nothing...

U.G.: Still that demand to do something is bound to be there.

Q : ...Which is the problem.

U.G.: That is the problem. You call it hopelessness and say, "Intellectually I understand". But that is the only way you can understand anything. That is what you are trying to do now. I can say that *that* [thought] is not the instrument, there is no other instrument, and there is nothing to understand. How this understanding dawned on me, I *really* don't know. If I knew that, it would be as worthless as any other thing. I really don't know. So, you have to be in a situation where you really don't know what to do about this whole situation. You have not exhausted the whole thing. You know, if you exhaust one, there is always another one [situation], another one, and yet another one.

Q : And even planing to exhaust that would be a disaster?

U.G.: Yes, to attempt to free yourself from that, to put yourself in a state that you really don't know, is part of the movement [of thought].

Leave The Body Alone

Q : Wherever you go people seem to comment on your demeanor and about your physical appearance. Yet I know you don't practice yoga or do any exercises.

U.G.: I don't exercise at all. The only walking I do is from my place to the post office, which is about half a kilometer or a quarter of a mile away from where I live. But I used to walk a lot.

Q : I remember that twenty years ago you used to take long walks. I have read that piece of information in one of your books.

U.G.: I am afraid that I may have to pay a heavy price for all the walking that I did before. You know, joking apart, I am not competent enough to offer any comments on these matters. But one thing I want to assert is that for some reason this body of ours does not want to know anything or learn anything from us. No doubt we have made tremendous advances in the field of medical technology. But are they really helping the body? That is one of the basic questions that we should ask.

Q : That is the question we always have to keep asking. Can we actually help the body?

U.G.: I think what we are actually doing is trying to treat the symptoms of what we call a disease. But my question is, and I always throw this question at the people who are competent enough – the doctors, what is health? What is disease? Is there any such thing as disease for this body? The body does not know that it is healthy or unhealthy. You know, we translate the 'malfunctioning' [of the body] to mean that there is some imbalance in the natural rhythm of the body. But we are so frightened that we run to a doctor or to somebody who we think is in the know of things and can help us. We do not give a chance to the body to work out the problems created by the situation we find ourselves in. We do not give enough time to the body. But what actually is health? Does the body know? Or does it have any way of knowing, that it is healthy or unhealthy?

Q : We do [know]. We translate health into the general terms of being free from having any symptoms. If I don't have a pain in my knee, then I don't have a disease there. We indulge in medical research in order to gather useful knowledge that could be applied when there is a pain in the knee.

U.G.: But what is pain? I am not asking a metaphysical question. To me pain is a healing process. But we do not give enough chance or opportunity to the body to heal itself or help itself, to free itself from what we call pain.

Q : You mean to say that we do not wait long enough so that the body can get rid of what we label as pain. We think pain is negative and then run here and there to get a remedy for it.

U.G.: We are frightened, you see. We are afraid that something terrible will happen to us.

Q : And that is where we become gullible. And this is being taken advantage of by some fakes and commercials.

U.G.: They are exploiting the gullibility and credulity of people. It is not that I am saying that you should not go to doctor or take the help of medicine. I am not one of those who believe that your prayers will help the body to recover from whatever disease it has, or that God is going to be the healer. Nothing like that. Pain is part of the biological functioning of the body, and that is all there is to it. And we have to rely or depend upon the chemistry of this body, and the body always gives us a warning. In the early stages we do not pay any attention, but when it becomes too much for the body to handle, there is panic and fear. Maybe it is necessary for us to go to a person who is in the know of affairs and get a helping hand from him. That's all we can do. The patient can be given a helping hand. All treatment, whether traditional or alternative, is based upon the account of the symptoms narrated by the patient.

Q : That's right.

U.G.: If it is a physical problem, you see, then it is a mechanical problem.

Q : Yes, but now a days, in the new medical school of

thought, there is a tendency to tell the doctors not listen to the patients too much and to do the tests themselves. But I think that is a mistake because if anybody knows, it's the patient who should know.

U.G.: But his anxiety is always colouring what he is telling you.

Q : That's true.

U.G.: But at the same time there is no other way than to depend upon what he is telling you. If somebody says he has this or that you have to go by what he says.

Q : But when you educate people, you give them some knowledge about how to help the body, and that would save them much anxiety when they have any pain.

U.G.: Do you mean to say that doctors are above all these problems? Doctors need more reassuring than others.

Q : Doctors too have pain in their knees.

U.G.: My advice to the doctors in that they should heal themselves first. It's so surprising that many of the heart specialists have died of heart failure.

Q : Yes, they have done some research on this. It's very interesting to learn that psychiatrists have tended to commit suicide more often than others.

U.G.: They do need psychiatric help.

Q : Do you know that cardiologists have more heart disease?

U.G.: Sure they do. There is a saying in India that a snake always bites the snake charmer, and that will be his end. It's very strange. He can get away with playing with the snake for a long time, but ultimately his end is always through the bite of a cobra or some other snake.

The basic problem is that we have unfortunately divided pain into physical and psychological pain. As I see it, there is no such thing as psychological pain at all. There is only physical pain.

Q : What about people who feel they are nervous or feel they have anxiety? That is why Valium is probably the most prescribed medication in this country.

U.G.: It puts you to sleep. When the physical pain is unbearable and you have no way of freeing yourself from it, the body becomes unconscious. In that unconscious state, if the body still has any chance of renewing itself to function normally, it tries to help itself. If it cannot, that's the end of the story. So the pain seems more acute than what it actually is because we are linking up all these sensations of pain and giving them continuity. Otherwise the pain is not so acute as we imagine it to be. Another problem is that we don't give a chance to the body to recuperate. We just run to the corner drugstore or a doctor and buy medicines. That's probably one of the things that are making it difficult for the body to handle its problems in its own way.

Q : When confronted with pain, the average person tries to take a shortcut.

U.G.: There is a shortcut because you have made tremendous progress in surgery.

Q : In fact, as you were saying, people can have injuries to their bodies from surgery or medication. Surgery sometimes makes the problem worse.

U.G.: All surgical corrections disturb the natural rhythm of the body. I am not for the moment saying that you should not take advantage of the tremendous strides made in the field of surgery. The basic question that we should all ask, "What for and why are we so eager to prolong life?" Now they are saying that it is possible for us to live beyond eighty-five. The dream of living for a hundred years, which has been the goal of every Indian, has come true. Every time you meet any elderly person there, he blesses you by saying, "May you live for a hundred years". But so far they have not succeeded. And in spite of the blessings of all the sages, saints, and saviours of mankind, the average age of an Indian has remained twenty-three-and-a-half years for centuries. But suddenly, I don't know why, it has jumped to fifty-three-and-odd years.

Q : What has happened there?

U.G.: Maybe it is because of the rich food they are eating.

Q : The death rate is also less. But people don't actually live longer in the older age groups.

U.G.: We place so much importance on the statistical truths of this, that, and the other. Statistics can be used either way. Either in favour or against someone's opinion.

Q : I want to refer to a bit more personal side of you. I have had lunch with you sometimes, and you eat vary little. I mean, the quantity of food you eat, when compared with the average in take of a person, is strikingly less. People are saying now that eating less food apparently increases the life span. In the case of animals they have found that out.

U.G.: As we grow older and older we have to reduce the quantity of the intake of food. We don't do that because our eating habits are based on nothing but pleasure. We eat for pleasure. Eating is a pleasure-seeking movement for us.

Q : There is a great variety of food that people are keen on.

U.G.: That is why in every television show I always make this very frivolous remark that if you like varieties of food, varieties of girls are also acceptable. That may be an antisocial activity, but it is acceptable to me - varieties of food, varieties of girls, or varieties of men. [Laughter] We eat more than what is necessary for the body. That is one of the basic things that we have to come to terms with. We don't need to eat so much food. I eat very little. I had many friends, top nutritionists, living with me as my neighbours in Chicago. For some reason, I have always been taking large quantity of cream - double cream, triple cream, clotted cream, name it. That's my basic food. They always warned me, "Look here, my good friend, we are very much interested that you should live long, but with this [eating of cream] you are going to have cholesterol problems. You will die of this, that, and the other". But I am still here, and they are all gone. I maintain that fat eats fat. [Laughter] Be that as it may, I am not recommending this [sort of diet] to anyone.

Q : I don't know whether you know the amount of calories you eat per day. It is probably something around six hundred to seven hundred calories a day.

U.G.: I have survived for seventy-three years.

Q : You are not weak. You look quite robust.

U.G.: It is very strange that ever since I was twenty-one my weight has remained one hundred and thirty-five pounds. It has never changed, regardless of what I eat or don't eat. That's the reason why I always emphasize, and it may sound very ridiculous to you, that you can live on sawdust and glue. The glue is just for adding flavour to the food!

Q : It is going to be very tasty some times....sure... [laughter]

U.G.: Instead of using curry powder or other spices you might as well use some glue. [Laughter] You know that's going too far, but nevertheless the fact does remain that those people who lived in concentration camps never had any trouble with their health.

Q : They have seen such things again and again in concentration camps. The American prisoners of war in Vietnam were healthy.

U.G.: Exactly. So it may sound very frivolous and ridiculous to say that, but when those people who had lived for years and years in concentration camps moved over to countries like the United States and Western Europe and ate this kind of food, they started having nothing but health problems. I am not making any generalization from that.

Q : You don't have a food fad. But the fact is that you eat very little quantity of food.

U.G.: Very little, you know. But I am not recommending this food to others at all. You know there are no hard and fast rules applicable to everyone. My suggestions to all these nutritionists and doctors is that they should rethink the matter and try to look at the functioning of this human body in a different way. But that will take a lot of jettisoning of our ideas that we have taken for granted.

Q : That is clearly necessary.

U.G.: Very necessary. But all those people who have tremendous investment in drugs and belong to the medical associations here and everywhere in the world will naturally oppose that suggestion. We have to look at things in a different way. We have to come to terms with the basic situation that this body of ours, which is the product of thousands and thousands years of evolution, has enough intelligence to help itself survive under any circumstances. All that it is interested in is its survival and reproduction. All the cultural inputs that you have imposed on this organism have absolutely no value for this body. It really does not want to learn or know anything from us. That being the situation, all the things that we are doing to help it to live longer, happier, and healthier are only creating problems for it. How long all this can go on I really don't know.

Q : You are saying that all the things we do are in some way or other probably hindering the body from living longer, healthier, and happier. So you must leave the body alone.

U.G.: Yes, leave the body alone. Don't get frightened and rush here, there, and everywhere. In any case, there is no way you can conquer death at all.

Q : I get what you say. People are trying subconsciously to prevent death.

U.G.: Our pushing people into a value system is a very undesirable thing, you know. You want to push everybody into a value system. We never question that this value system, which we have cherished for centuries, may be the very thing that is responsible for our misery.

Q : Yes, that may be the very thing that is generating disease.

U.G.: Disease and conflict in our lives. We really don't know. Another thing I want to emphasize is that what we call identity, the 'I', the 'me', the 'you', the 'center', the 'psyche', is artificially created. It does not exist at all.

Q : It is also a cultural phenomenon.

U.G.: Yes, it has been culturally created. We are doing everything possible to maintain that identity, whether we are asleep, awake, or dreaming. The instrument that we use to maintain this identity strengthens, fortifies, and gives continuity to it. The constant use of memory is wearing you out. We really do not know what memory is, but we are constantly using it to maintain that non-existent identity of ours.

Q : You are saying that we are constantly using our memory to remind ourselves that we are individuals.

U.G.: We really don't know, and nobody has come up with any definite and positive answer to the question of what memory is. You may say it is all neurons, but there is this constant use of memory to maintain identity.

Q: Memory is a major problem now because people are literally losing it.

U.G.: That's what we call Alzheimer's disease; and that is going to be the fate of mankind. You may kid yourself and tell everybody that it is caused by the use of aluminum vessels and all that...

Q: But why do you say that it is the fate of mankind?

U.G.: Because it [memory] is consuming tremendous amounts of energy.

Q: Everyone in using memory all the time never-endingly.

U.G.: A certain amount of the use of memory is absolutely essential; but to use it to live forever, to be fit and to be healthier, will create complications.

Q: But you have to remember to go home, and you have to use your memory for that.

U.G.: That is part of the living organism. That's already there. Animals have that kind of memory.

Q: Right, an animal knows how to get back to its home. But that's not the kind of memory you are talking about.

U.G.: No. It is that [memory which maintains our identity] that is responsible for turning us all into neurotic individuals. The constant use of that is going to be the tragedy of mankind. Because of this overuse we don't have enough energy to deal with the problems of living. It is consuming tremendous amounts of energy. But there are no hard and fast rules, so much so that anybody can offer us ways and means of freeing ourselves from this danger that we are all going to face one of these days.

Q : So you are saying in a sense that memory is almost like a muscle that is wearing out. It is being worn out by constant use.

U.G.: Yes. I maintain that there is some neurological disorder in the nervous system.

Q : Is it in the form of a complaint that we have to remember too many numbers or store too much infor-mation?

U.G.: Now with the help of the computers it is easy for us to use less and less of our memory [for those purpose].

Q : You think so? But it seems that the computers somehow have made the problem even more complex. They have not really helped people.

U.G.: I think they have. I have a word-finder that is very helpful. There was a time when we were made to memorize dictionaries, the thesaurus of Sanskrit, and all that. But now there is no need. You jus t press a button, the machine says, "Searching", and a little latter it tells you the meaning of the word, as well as its root meaning and spelling. It is a lot easier to use such machines than to memorize all that information.,Our reliance on memory [for those purposes] will very soon be unnecessary.

Q : Well, if that could be done, that will certainly relieve us of a lot of problems.

U.G.: One of these days you will be out of your job!

Q : That will be fine...

U.G.: ... Because the computer will analyze all your symptoms and tell you what to do. And the robots will take the place of specialist-surgeons and perform operations. I suggest that you should make enough money and retire before such an event occurs. [Laughter]

Q : You said that one should look at the body entirely differently. Here they are trying to look at the pineal gland.

U.G.: They call that *ajna chakra* in India. We don't want to use those Sanskrit words.

Q : Twenty years ago they were saying in America that this gland had no use. They now find that the gland actually creates...

U.G.: They have to revise all their opinions and ideas about these glands. Because of the constant use of the memory, which is thought, to maintain identity, many of these glands, which are very essential for the functioning of the living organism, have remained dormant, inert, and inactive. Some people who are interested in religious things try to activate them, and feel that they are getting somewhere. But if you try to activate any of those through some techniques that you are importing from countries like India or elsewhere, it might be dangerous. They [those techniques] might shatter the whole nervous system. Instead of helping people, they might just give you a 'high'. One danger in playing with these glands is that we might create more problems for this body rather than to help it function normally, sanely, and intelligently. That danger is there.

Q : That [trying to activate these glands] somehow will generate a whole series of problems.

U.G.: Yes. Say, for example, the pituitary gland. They say (I don't know this myself) that it is responsible for the height of the body. Through manipulation or activation of that gland, you can grow taller.

Q : Exactly, you are given growth hormones.

U.G.: Yes, growth hormones. It's good for the research scientists to indulge in such things, and they will be amply rewarded by the society. But we don't know whether they are really helping us. There is not enough research done on these things, and it may be highly dangerou s to rush into doing something with them.

Q : What do you think about the pineal gland?

U.G.: That is the most important gland. That is why they called it the *ajna chakra* in Sanskrit.

Q : It is injured by thought, yet they are using thought to investigate it.

U.G.: Yes. They are not going to succeed. Probably they will use it for healing purposes or ...

Q : But what most people are doing is actually injuring their own pineal gland.

U.G.: Exactly. If it is activated in a natural way, it will take over and give directions to the functioning of this body without thought interfering all the time.

Q : So we keep coming back to this point that thought itself seems to be the enemy, the interloper.

U.G.: It is our enemy. Thought is a protective mechanism. It is interested in protecting itself at the expense of the living organism.

Q : You are saying that thought is the thing that causes people's worries.

U.G.: It's thought that is crating all our problems, and it is not the instrument to help us solve the problems created by itself.

It's Terror, Not Love, That Keeps Us Together

Q : After reflecting on some of the things you have said, a few questions have arisen in my mind which I would like, if I may, to discuss with you over the next few days.

U.G.: Yes, Sir.

Q : You talk of a state that is entirely natural to man. I want to know if that natural state can be acquired by effort- if it can be acquired at all - or is it simply a chance occurrence?

U.G.: When I use the term 'natural state' it is not a synonym for 'enlightenment', 'freedom', or 'God-realization', and so forth. Not at all. When the totality of mankind's knowledge and experience loses its stranglehold on the body – the physical organism – then the body is allowed to function in its own harmonious way. Your natural state is a biological, neurological, and physical state.

Q: Then I presume that you agree with modern science that it is the genes that control our behaviour and destinies.

U.G.: I can make no definitive statements about the part genes play in the evolutionary process, but at the moment it appears that Darwin was at least partially wrong in insisting that acquired characteristics could not be genetically transmitted. I think that they *are* transmitted in some fashion. I am not competent enough to say whether the genes play any part in the transmission.

Anyway, the problem lies in our psyche. We function in a thought-sphere, and not in our biology. The separative thought structure, which is the totality of man's thoughts, feelings, experiences, and so on - what we call psyche or soul or self – is creating the disturbance. That is what is responsible for our misery; that's what continues the battle that is going on there [in the human being] all the time. This interloper, the thought sphere, has created your entire value system. The body is not in the least interested in values, much less a value system. It is only concerned with intelligent moment-to-moment *survival*, and nothing else. Spiritual 'values' have no meaning to it. When, through some miracle or chance, you are freed from the hold of thought and culture, you are left with the body's natural functions, and nothing else. It then functions without the interference of thought. Unfortunately, the servant, which is the thought structure that is there, has taken possession of the house. But he can no longer control and run the household. So he must be dislodged. It is in this sense that I use the term 'natural state', without any connotation of spirituality or enlightenment.

Q : As a scientist I can only allow myself to be interested in things which I can predict and control through experimentation. I must be able to repeat the results of another scientist; if not, I must, in the name of sound science, reject what he says, and his so-called evidence. So, I am tempted to ask whether someone can demonstrate that state to me, whether it is possible to reproduce it.

U.G.: That is the very thing I am against. Nature does not use models. No two leaves are the same; no two human beings are the same. I understand your problem. You are not the first scientist to come here demanding 'scientific proof', throwing questions at me like, "Why can't we test these statements you are making". First of all, I am not selling anything. Second, their interest and yours, is to use this natural state in your misguided efforts to change or 'save' mankind. *I say that no change is necessary, period.* Your corrupt society has put into you this notion of change, that you are this and you must be that. Anything that insists that you be something other then what you in fact are is the very thing that is falsifying you and the world. I somehow stumbled into this natural state on my own, and I cannot, under any circumstances transmit it to others. It has no social, political, commercial, or transformational value to anyone. I do not sit upon platforms haranguing you, demanding that you change the world. As things are, you and the world -which are not two separate things - cannot be any different. All these attempts on the part of man to change himself go entirely against the way nature is operating. That is why I am not interested. Sorry! Take it or leave it. It's up to you. Whether you praise me or insult me I am not in the least interested. It is your affair. I don't fit into the picture [of 'scientific investigation'] at all. I am only talking about it in response to your questions. You throw the ball, and it bounces back. There is no urge in me to express myself to you or anyone else.

Q: Although you don't talk about designing a perfect culture or society, as B.F. Skinner does in *Beyond Freedom and Dignity*, you too seem to emphasize the importance of culture in guiding mankind's destiny...

U.G.: Did I say so in that book of mine? I don't even know what there is in that book... Culture is a way of life and the way of thinking of a people. To me, this is culture: how we entertain ourselves, how we speculate about reality, what kind of things we are interested in, what kind of art we have, so on. Whether the culture is Oriental or Occidental, it is basically the same. I don't see any difference between the two except one of accent, just as we all speak English with different accents. All human beings are exactly the same, whether they are Russian, American or Indian. What is going on in the head of that man walking in the street is no different from what is going on inside the head of a person walking in a street in New York. Basically it is the same. His goal may be different. But the instrument he is using to achieve his goal is exactly the same, namely, his trying to become something other than what he is.

I am not interested in helping anyone... Things have gone too far. If, just to take one example, the evermore-sophisticated genetic engineering techniques are monopolized by the state, we are sunk. What little freedom is still open to mankind will be brought under the control of the state, and the state will be in a position to create designer human beings, any type it wants, with impunity. It is all very respectable. Mankind will be robotized on a scale never dreamt before. What can be done to stop or prevent that sort of catastrophe? I say, nothing. It is too late. You may call me a skeptic, a cynic, a this or a that, but this is hard realism. It is your privilege to think what you will, but I fail to see any way out, as long as man remains as he is, which is almost a certainty. I don't see how it is possible for us to reverse this trend.

This crisis has not arrived unannounced. It has been building up for a long time, from the day man felt this self-consciousness in himself, and decided that the world was created for him to hold and rule. On that day he laid the foundation for the total destruction of everything that nature has taken so many millennia to create and build.

Q : But behind the change of nature there seems to be some kind of plan or purpose, don't you think?

U.G.: I don't see any plan or scheme there at all! There is a process - I wouldn't necessarily call it evolution - but when it slows down then a revolution takes place. Nature tries to put together something and start all over again, just for the sake of creating. This is the only true creativity. Nature uses no models or precedents, and so has nothing to do with art *per se*.

Artists find it comforting to think that they are creative: 'creative art', 'creative ideas', and 'creative politics'. It's nonsense. There is nothing really creative in them in the sense of doing anything original, new or free. The artists pick something here and something there, put them together, and think they have created something marvellous. They are using something that is already there; their work is an imitation. Only, they are not decorous enough to admit that. They are all imitating something that is already there. Imitation and style are the only 'creativity' we have. We each have our own style according to the school we attended, the language we are taught, the books we have read, and the examinations we have taken. And within that framework again we each have our own style. Perfecting style and technique is all that operates there.

Q : Still, we must admit that some artists can produce things of power and beauty...

U.G.: The framing of what there is by the mind is what you call beauty. Beauty is [in] the frame[ing]. The framing creates the conclusion, the thought, which it then calls beauty. Otherwise there is no beauty at all. Beauty is not in the object. Nor is it in the eye of the beholder. To say, like the Upanishads do, that the total absence of the self is beauty is a lot hogwash! The act of capturing and framing, which thought creates for us, is what we call beauty. Perhaps I am going off on a tangent....

Q : No, no, you are helping me immensely. What you say is of great use to me. I am integrating your statements within myself as we go along... Don't think that what you say is useless.

U.G.: You want to make something of what I am saying, to use it somehow to further your own aims. You may say that it is for humanity's sake, but really you don't give a damn about society at all. What I am saying cannot possibly be of any use to you or your society. It can only put an end to you us you know yourself now.

Neither is what I am saying of any use of me because I cannot set up any holy business and make money. It is just impossible for me. I am not interested in freeing anyone or taking anybody from his or her *gurus*. You can go to the temples and pray there. You certainly get some comfort. You need to be comforted: that is what you want. And they provide you with that. This is a wrong place to come. Go anywhere you want. I have no interest in freeing you at all. I don't even *believe* in altering you in any way, or saving or reforming society, or doing anything for mankind.

Q : But there seems to be some sort of underlying

motive, an all-pervasive demand, that seems to distort and frustrate society's efforts to bring about order.

U.G.: It is the constant demand for permanence that cripples the society. Because we all seek permanence inwardly, we demand that those things, which we perceive to lie outside ourselves – society, humanity, the nation, and the world – also be permanent. We seek our permanence through them. All forms of permanence, whether personal or collective, are your own creation. They are all an extension of the very same demand for permanence. But nothing is permanent. Our efforts to make things permanent go entirely against the way of nature. Somehow you know that you will not succeed in your demand for permanence. Yet you persist.

Q : Still, for most of us, many questions remain. We want to somehow find out what life is, if it has any meaning.

U.G.: Life is something, which you cannot capture, contain, and give expression to. Energy is an expression of life. What is death? It is simply a condition of the human body. There is no such thing as death. What you have are ideas about death, ideas that arise when you sense the absence of another person. Your own death, or the death of your near and dear ones, is not something you can experience. What you actually experience is the void created by the disappearance of another individual, and the unsatisfied demand to maintain the continuity of your relationship with that person for a non-existent eternity. The arena for the continuation of all these 'permanent' relationships is the tomorrow – heaven, next life, and so on. These things are the inventions of a mind interested only in its undisturbed, permanent continuity in a 'self'-generated, fictitious future. The basic method of maintaining the continuity is the incessant repetition of the question, "How? How? How?" "How am I to live? How can I be happy? How can I be sure I will be happy tomorrow?" This has made life an insoluble dilemma for us. We want to *know*, and through that knowledge we hope to continue on with our miserable existences forever.

Q : So many people in this society are interested in...

U.G.: Society cannot be interested in what I am talking about. Society is, after all, two individuals or a thousand of them put together. Because I am a direct threat to you individually – as you know and experience yourself – I am also a threat to society. How can society possibly be interested in this sort of thing? Not a chance. Society is the sum of relationships, and despite what you may find agreeable to believe, all these relationships are sordid and horrible. This is the unsavory fact; take it or live it. You cannot help but superimpose over these horrible ugly relationships a soothing fictitious veneer of "loving", "compassionate", " brotherly", and "harmonious" or some other fancy relationships.

Q : So, it is possible, in the here and now, to brush aside the demand for perfect, permanent relationships, and deal with our actual relationships. Is that it?

U.G.: No, sorry! All this talk of "here and now", much less a "here and now" within which you can solve all your miseries, is, for me, pure bunk. All you know is separateness and duration, space and time, which is the 'frame' superimposed by the mind over the flow of life. But anything that happens in space and time is limiting the energy of life. What life is I don't know; nor will I ever. You can say that life is this, that, or the other, and give hundreds of definitions. But the definitions do not capture life. It's like a flowing river. You take a bucket full of water from it, analyze it into its constituent elements, and say that the river is the same [as the bucketful of water]. But the quality of flow is absent in the water in the bucket. So, as the Zen proverb says: "You can never cross the same river twice". It's flowing all the time.

You cannot talk of life or of death because life has no beginning or end, period. You can say there is life because you are responding to stimuli. But what happens after you are dead? The word 'dead' is only a definition – a condition of your body. The body itself, after what is called clinical death, no longer responds to stimuli the way in which we know it now. It is probably still responding in some fashion: the brain waves continue for a long time after clinical death takes place.

Through your death you are giving continuity to life, or whatever you call it. I can't say you are dead: only that you are not useful to me any more. If you bury a dead body, something is happening there; if you burn the body, the ashes are enriching the soil; if you throw it in water, the fish will eat it; if you leave it there in the vulture-pit, the vultures will eat it. You are providing the means for the continuity of life.

So, you can't say the body is dead. It is not metaphysics that I am talking about here. It is only your fear of something coming to an end that is the problem. Do you want to be free from that fear? I say, "No." The ending of fear is the ending of you as you know yourself. I am not talking of the psychological, romantic death of "dying to your yesterdays". That body of yours, I assure you, drops dead on the spot the moment the continuity of knowledge is broken.

Q : But as a scientist I ask myself, what are my obligations to my fellow beings?

U.G.: None whatsoever... Sorry. All you are interested in as a scientist is self-fulfillment, the ultimate goal of a Nobel Prize, and power. I am very sorry. Personally, you may not be interested in that kind of thing. That's all. I encourage that kind of pursuit. Of course, you scientists have made all this comfort-bearing technology possible, and in that sense, I, like all those who enjoy the benefits of modern technology, am indeed indebted. I don't want to go back to the days of the spinning wheel and the bullock cart. That would be too silly, too absurd. Pure science is nothing but speculation. The scientists discuss formulas endlessly and provide us with some equations. But I am not at all taken in by the "march of progress" and all that rot. The first trip I made to the U.S. in the thirties took more than a full day; we had to stop everywhere. Later, the same trip took eighteen hours, then twelve hours, and even more recently six hours and three, and so on. And if the supersonic jets are put to commercial use we may be able to make the trip in one-and-a-half hours.

All right, that's progress. But the same technology that makes fast international travel possible is making ever more deadly military fighter planes. How many of these planes are we using for faster and more comfortable travel from one point to another? And how many more hundreds of planes are we using to destroy life and property? You call this progress? I don't know. As the comforts increase, we come to depend upon them, and are loath to give up anything we have.

Within a particular frame I say it is progress. I am now living in an air-conditioned room. My grandfather used a servant who sat in the hot sun and pulled the *punkha*, and before that we used a palm leaf hand fan. As we move in to more and more comfortable situations we don't want to give up anything.

Q : But surely some have too much and should give up some of...

U.G.: Why do you expect others to give up all they have? The poor man there is not ready to give up his tiny little hut, and you expect all the rich men to give up all their mansions. No, they are just not going to do that. They will fight to their last breath to protect what they have, and kill themselves in the process. That is inevitable. What do wild animals do? They at first try to flee, then fight until they kill each other.

Q : Sir, I would like to ask you two connected questions...

U.G.: I am myself disconnected and disjointed...

Q : I will do the integrating...

U.G.: All right. Anyway, it is through you that I can express myself. You are the medium of my expression.

Q : I am interested in finding out why we pursue knowledge. Is it for knowledge's sake, or for the sake of mankind, or with some other motive?

U.G.: Power!

Q : Power?

U.G.: Power. I am sorry. There is no such thing as knowledge for knowledge's sake or art for art's sake. It is certainly not for the benefit of mankind. Knowledge gives me power: "I know and you don't know". Sir, if I may ask, what is your specialty?

Q : I am a sort of jack-of-all-trades and master of none.I was trained in organic chemistry. Then I went to the university medical school, and worked in the field of cancer chemotherapy. I am now doing research in genetic e ngineering. It has trem endous possibilities.

U.G.: I see, that is your field…

Q : It's not my field. But I am fascinated by it.

U.G.: I may be wrong, but I feel, Sir, that man's problems, even his psychological problems, can only be solved through the help of his genes. If they can show that the tendency, say, to steal, is genetically determined, where will that leave us? It implies that man has no freedom of action in any area. Even the capacity to learn a language is also genetically determined. The genes control the whole thing; every tendency, capacity, and kind of behaviour. Man has no freedom of action. His wanting and demanding freedom of action seems to be the cause of his suffering. I am not at all proposing the fatalistic philosophy that people preach in this country. My emphasis is quite different. So, shall we go back to the question of genetics?

Q : Should we, then, pursue aggressive research in the field? The field offers great possibilities.

U.G.: Whether you like it or not, they are going to do it. You have no say in the matter. If you don't do it someone else will. How can you stop it? Any schoolboy knows how they make an atom bomb. And on a worldwide basis, huge amount of fissionable materials are already missing. They will end up in God-knows-whose hands. The know-how is available to everyone. One day someone is going to use it. Then we will be in trouble. If you don't do it [the research], because you are prevented by some ethical code, it's not going to work, because the code won't prevent someone else.

Q : No, I think we can control it.

U.G.: Yes, but for how long?

Q : Well, just as long as we can...

U.G.: Postpone the evil day? Is that it? That's all we are trying to do. But for whose benefit? I am not singing a gloomy song of doom. If mankind goes, I am ready to go with it. But what can we do about it? There isn't a thing we can do. It is too far-gone.

Q : At times I wonder whether we took a wrong route...

U.G.: I don't think that we deliberately took the wrong path. Something happened long ago to the human race. We are now a menace to the planet. Perhaps it is nature's way to clear away and start afresh in the fastest way. I don't see any scheme in nature, do you? We project our own ideations and mentations on to nature and imagine it to be sweetly ordered. We imagine that there is a scheme or plan, and such a things as evolution. I don't see any such thing. There may be no evolution except what we see in nature and what we project onto it. By putting things together we surmise that *that* has evolved from *this*.

Q : But there seem to be anomalies and exceptions in nature...

U.G.: Somewhere along the line the process slows down.

And when it does, then it takes a leap. This we call a mutation. Is there any relation between the two? Seeking to find a scheme behind it all, we link up these two things and call it evolution. It is the same in physics.

So, what do we do? I don't have the answer. It is not given to me. No one has chosen or elected me to be the saviour of mankind. All this talk of a permanent, eternal, perfect mankind has absolutely no meaning to me. I am interested only in the way we are functioning right now.

It [the body] is not thinking in terms of a hundred years, or two hundred yeas, or even tomorrow. No, it is only interested in survival now. If it is confronted with danger, it throws in everything it has, that is, all its resources, to survive in that particular situation. If it survives that moment, then the next moment is there for it. That is its own reward: to go on living for one more moment. This is the way the body is functioning now. Don't bother inventing philosophies of the moment, situational models, and all that. The body functions from moment to moment because the sensory perceptions and responses to the stimuli are also from moment to moment. Each perception or response is independent. What the purpose of the body is, why it is there, where it all may be heading, I really don't know. I have no way of finding out. If you think you know, then good luck to you!

So, why bother trying to stop the growth of genetic engineering? Tell me.

Q: No, I am merely wondering whether we are taking the right step and in the right direction?

U.G.: So, what is the motivation behind all this research? Tell me.

Q : I would like to think that it is the healthy pursuit of knowledge, for the satisfaction of curiosity, and for the sheer enjoyment for it.

U.G.: But it doesn't stop there.

Q : True. Other people, politicians and the like, exploit our results.

U.G.: I am afraid you cannot so easily exonerate the scientists themselves. Einstein encouraged Roosevelt to drop the atom bomb. "If you don't do it, they will", he said. Out of his contempt for Germany and gratitude to the United States, which helped him flourish in his work and produce tremendous results, he gave that advice. He came to regret that advice later on. That doesn't matter.

Q : Yes, but as a scientist I think we have to balance the costs, risks, and benefits of everything we do. I am a chemist. I am afraid we chemists have a rather poor reputation for polluting the atmosphere. But our intention was not to pollute the atmosphere...

U.G.: Don't you think that pollution goes hand in hand with your research? Where do you draw the line?

Q : That is difficult, very difficult to say.

U.G.: These environmental problems have been allowed to escalate into huge crises, so huge that in fact they are beyond what any individual or even ecologists can tackle any more. Look out of the window. Observe the sickening fumes, the poisonous air. The factories are pumping out millions of tons, of deadly wastes.

There is more pollution here than in Western countries. To clean up the exhaust fumes from all the contaminating chemicals takes huge amounts of money. These companies are not going to voluntarily clean up the mess. Do you think General Motors and the others give a damn? If I had any shares in a company, and I don't actually, I would want dividends, not a bill for clean-up costs. Any management team that advocated corporate responsibility would be run out of office at once. As a shareholder I would want income, period. I wouldn't give a damn for all the people, animals, and plants that are there.

Now it as become fashionable to become an ecologist. Prince Philip's talk of saving the whales is a joke to me. And Queen Anne talks of saving the seals! Why are they concerned about whales and seals? If what I read is true, only fifteen percent of all the animal species that ever lived are alive today. All the other species have become extinct. Only five percent of all the plant species that ever existed exist now. So, extinction of species is the regular order of things in nature. Perhaps man should have become extinct long ago. I don't know. It's too late now. This one species alone is increasing the rate of extinction of all other species beyond what could have been thought possible. The self-consciousness in the human species, the idea that the world was created for man alone, is the real problem. The useless ecologists, form groups, attend meetings, collect funds, start foundations, build organizations worth millions with presidents and vice-presidents, and they all make money. It may sound very cynical to you, but the fact of the matter is that they have no real power. The solutions do not lie with them. The problem is out of their hands. Governments have the power to do something, but they are not interested.

Q: But the scientific community is not without influence...

U.G.: No, sorry. You may call me a cynic, but the cynic is a realist who has his feet firmly planted in the ground. You don't want to look at the reality of the situation.

Q : Some would argue that a humanity restored not through science but through love is our only hope.

U.G.: I still maintain that it is not love, compassion, humanism, or brotherly sentiments that will save mankind. No, not at all. It is the sheer terror of extinction that can save us, if anything can. Each cell of a living organism cooperates with the cell next to it. It does not need any sentiment or declarations of undying love to do so. Each cell is wise enough to know that if its neighbour goes, it also goes. The cells stick together not out of brotherhood, love and that kind of thing, but out of the urgent drive to survive.

It is the same with us, but only in a larger scale. Soon we will all come to know one simple thing: if I try to destroy you, I will also be destroyed. We see the superpowers of today signing arms control pacts, rushing to sign no-first-strike accords, and the like. Even the big bully boys, who have among them controlled the world's resources, no longer talk about a winnable nuclear war. Even the arrogant, swashbuckling United States has changed its tune. It no longer talks - as it did twenty years ago under Dulles and other cold warriors - of massive retaliation. If you read the *Time* magazine now, it doesn't talk about the United States as the mightiest, the richest, the most powerful, and the most invincible of all nations. It refers to it as "one of the superpowers".

Q : But the United States is the only country that has actually used 'the Bomb' in war. There is no guarantee that ...

U.G.: I don't trust the Americans. If America were on the losing side in a big war, then what it would do is anybody's guess. I am not personally alarmed or concerned at all: if the Americans want to blow up the world, I am ready to go with them and with the rest of the world. But that's not the point. I am reasonably convinced that the Russians won't blow up the world. They have already suffered so much: they know the firsthand the horrors of war. They were invaded and they lost twenty million of their citizens, while Americans lost few lives, gained immense power as a result of the war, and sacrificed only some of its natural resources. Hitler created full employment in the U.S. overnight.

America showered bombs on the poor Vietnamese at a cost of $101 billion. It is that war that shattered the dollar. Each time that Vietnamese fellow walking in flip-flops brought down with his Tommy gun planes worth millions and millions of dollars, it was not just the paper greenback money that was lost, but also all those material resources of the earth.

Here in India it is the same story. We still call this a non-violent nation! It's a joke to me. What do we do, Sir?

You scientists are the ones who control the fate of the world, not these *gurus*, not these religious people. The fate of the world is in your hands and not in the hands of government. But your research funds have to come from them. They hold the strings. So, what do we do? The situation is so horrible. What do we do? I want to know. But sill we play with each other: "Who has an edge over whom in the world?"

Q : Surely good deeds are possible despite our drive for power?

U.G.: What good deeds?

Q : Anything, like a simple act of planting a coconut tree...

U.G.: But the chap who planted the tree is not going to eat its fruit. Some future generations are going to enjoy it. You think it's the same thing, because you feel good about the continuity you will have with them. I am not saying anything against it. Lay the roads, dig the tunnels and all that for future generations... I am only pointing out that there may not be anyone left to enjoy all those fine things!

Q : What I am trying to understand is: is he doing it with good intentions or is it power that prompts him?

U.G.: Why are you doing what you are doing? If I put that question to you what is your answer?

Q : Are my actions perhaps due to my desire for power?

U.G.: You tell me. I don't have an answer.

Q : I always delude myself.

U.G.: Exactly, that is what I am trying to point out. There is nothing wrong about it. I am on your side. Do what you have to, but don't conveniently place it under the fabric of humanitarianism, brotherly love, self-sacrifice, and such other comforting ideas. At the same time I am telling you that the fate of the planet is in the hands of today's scientists, not in the hands of the mystics and holymen, who come talking of changing the world, of creating a heaven on earth. It is these ideas, full of absolute and poetic fancy, that have turned this place into a hell. I have entrusted the whole thing to the scientists. So, tell me. What are you going to do?

Q : I am pleased that you harbour so much faith in the scientific community.

U.G.: I have more faith in you and your colleagues than in all these people that are going around 'saving' mankind. We need to be saved from the self-appointed saviours of mankind. They are the ones who are responsible for the terrible situation we find ourselves in today. We don't realize that it is they who have created this mess for us. They had their day, and have utterly, totally failed. Still they refuse to take a back seat. That's it. We are stuck. You study the history of mankind: monarchies, revolutions, democracies, and more revolutions. Everything has failed us; everything is over. Not one ideology will survive. What's left for us? Democracy, the 'noble experiment', is over. Everything is over. We find ourselves in a situation where your boss will decide these issues.

Take the problem of starvation. One side says, "*My* political system will solve the problem of starvation in this world", and the other side says, "No, *mine* will"; and both of them end up on the battlefield brandishing their atomic weapons. That is the reality of the situation. Everywhere, on every continent, there is confrontation.

The basic issue in the world is, of course, economic: who will control the resources of this world? The nine rich nations of the world have been so used to controlling the resources of the world. They sit in Basel, Switzerland, and say, "Here is the price you must take for your products. Take it or leave it". A country like United States may talk of freedom, democracy, and justice, but they would like to have military governments in countries like those of South America. They prefer to do business with militarized, authoritarian states. A military general is very useful to run those countries. That is a fact.

Who or what can save you from all this? Not I, you may be sure. I am not a saviour of mankind. I don't even want to save you. You can stay in heaven or hell as the case may be... The fact is you already are in hell, and seem to enjoy it. Good luck to you!

Q: Somehow I do feel a responsibility to my fellow beings, not in a philosophical or spiritual sense, but in a more fundamental sense. You see someone starving, and you would like to do something about it.

U.G.: As an individual you can. But the moment you start an institution, and the institutions try to enlist individuals' help, and then the whole thing is destroyed. You have to organize, and there is no other way. That means my plan and your plan. It means war. Look at Mother Teresa. What is going on there? As an individual, she did a tremendous amount of service. But now she is only interested in the money – meeting the heads of governments and collecting money everywhere. I am glad they are stealing the money from the envelopes that pour in. The money ends up in a Hong Kong bank: have you heard the news?

Q: You see, as a scientist I feel an individual responsibility.

U.G.: To whom?

Q: To what I do.

U.G.: What you do is really an expression of your urge for self-fulfillment. You may not agree. What is it that you are trying to do there? You say your actions are very noble, meant to help the suffering world. Not a chance. You are only interested in your Nobel Prize, and the recognition it brings. How are you going to solve individually these immense problems of the world? Only through governments. There is no other way. And they are at each other's throat and armed to the teeth. Individually there isn't anything that you can do. Not a damn thing! You have so many conventions of scientists. What do they say?

Q : We feel that collectively we can do something; otherwise the future for the world is bleak indeed.

U.G.: Doing something collectively means war... It's like the European Economic Community. Each one has their own idea of running their country. Each country wants its own language, its own laws, its own king or queen, and resents any interference in its affairs from other countries. They have however; set aside these differences in order to solve larger problems. But individually what can you do? Why are you concerned about humanity?

Q : As you would say, the urge to help is a result of my culture. When you see someone sad, tears come to your eyes. We empathize...

U.G.: We translate that as sadness, and the tears follow as a sentimental effect. But the tear ducts are there to protect your eyes from going blind, to keep them lubricated and cleansed, and not to respond to the suffering of others. This may be a crude way of putting things, but that's the fact of the matter.

Q : Tears are also an expression of sadness...

U.G.: We have translated that as an expression of sadness. Emotions activate the glands, unfortunately....

Q : You see, we have difficulty in understanding the

ethical implications of our actions. In our zeal and enthusiasm to do something...

U.G.: The ethical considerations are what are standing in the way of your doing something. You don't have the energy to deal with this problem because you are throwing away what energy you do have by including in all these pointless ethical considerations. Otherwise you would find some way of neutralizing the whole thing. There must be some way of doing it. The superpowers will soon be humbled, neutralized in no time, by a single terrorist. Gaddaffi needs only one atomic hand grenade to neutralize the power of the mighty nations. They say that they already have a hand grenade that can blow up the Golden Gate Bridge. I wouldn't know. We now have hydrogen bombs, gas warfare – horrible weapons at our disposal. Look at the billions being poured into these arms. What for?

Q: Even worse than the atomic grenades is the biological warfare. It's terrible.

U.G.: That's the worst. You don't even need that. They have those atom bombs piling up. Yet they have no use for them. What huge amounts of money we are pouring into that! What for?

Q: If someone drops an atom bomb it is obvious. We can see it. But biological warfare is something that can be carried on in a subtle way without anyone discovering what's going on ... I must be leaving soon. But I would like to put to you one more question some what unrelated to what we have been discussing: what is your opinion regarding the existence of God?

U.G.: Oh my God! You really want my answer? To me the

question of whether God exists or not is irrelevant and immaterial. We have no use for God. We have used God to justify the killing of millions and millions of people. We exploit God.

Q : That's the negative aspect of it.

U.G.: That's the positive aspect of it, not the negative. In the name of God we have killed more people than in the two world wars put together. In Japan millions of people died in the name of the sacred Buddha. Here in India, five thousand Jains were massacred in a single day. This is not a peaceful nation! You don't want to read your own history: it's full of violence from the beginning to the end.

Q : Then how can people remain as a group if they don't believe in something?

U.G.: The fear of extinction will probably bring us together, not 'love' or feeling of brotherhood. The invention of God, along with all those other beliefs, may have served mankind's instinct to survive for some time in the past, but not now. It's the extension of the same survival mechanism that now operates through the fear of extinction. The biological instinct is very powerful, and the fear of extinction. The biological instinct is very powerful, and the fear of extinction, not love and compassion, will probably be the saviour of mankind.

SMRITI BOOKS

HINDOO STORIES

(Collected and collated by Anaryan)

160 pages, 140 × 215 mm
ISBN No: 81-87967-02-1

Since the beginning of humanity, fables and stories have been the means of imparting instruction and amusement to man. The stories were designed to illustrate and exemplify precept for human conduct. After centuries, these stories eventually found themselves in print. They are divided into four groups: Sanskrit or Hindoo, Arabic or Persian, Western or European and the American. Of these, the Sanskrit or Hindoo groups of stories are the oldest and probably served as the basis of Arabic or Persian fables, which again served as the source for many European storytellers.

BAITAL PACHCHISI

(Retold by John Platts)

192 pages, 140 × 215 mm
ISBN No: 81-87967-01-3

Among the many tales popular in India, one collection of stories has been existing not only in Sanskrit, but also in almost all the vernaculars. This is the BAITAL PACHCHISI, or Twenty-Five Tales of A Demon (or Sprite). They are narrated by the sprite, who haunts the cemeteries, to Vikram, the king of Oojein. JOHN PLATTS is among the first six to translate this collection into English from the original Sanskrit.

INDIAN MYTH AND LEGEND

(Written by Donald. A. Mackenzie)

586 pages, 140 × 215 mm
ISBN No: 81-87967-02-1

This book deals with the myths and legends of India, which survive in the rich and abundant storehouse of Sanskrit literature. The reader is introduced to the various sacred works of the Hindus. The ancient forest sages and poets of India invested the legendary themes and traditional beliefs with beautiful symbolism and used them as mediums for speculative thought and profound spiritual teaching. These ennobling ideas are still a potent culturing influence in the domestic, social and religious lives of millions of Indians.

DELHI: A TALE OF SEVEN CITIES

(Written by Urmila Varma)

125 pages, 140 × 225 mm
ISBN No: 81-87967-04-8

The story of the city of Delhi has a Phoenix like characteristic and phenomenal magnetism. The book narrates the seven cities as Lalkot and Kila Rai Pithora, as the first city of Delhi, moving on to Siri, Tughlaqabad, Jahanpanh, Firozabad, Dinpanah and Shahjahanabad. Buffeted by monarchic and dynastic changes, the city of Delhi still preserves glimpses of the past memories. The book is an attempt to revive those memories.

THE COURAGE TO STAND ALONE

(Conversations with U.G. Krishnamurti)

Foreword by Mahesh Bhatt

126 pages, 140 × 215 mm

ISBN No: 81-87967-06-4

There is some compelling purity about him, some way in which he captures a kind of longing that we all seem to have for a genuinely wise human being.

No one in the history of the world has had the courage to blast authority the way he has and yet no one has stared at one's own insignificance as boldly in the eye.

THOUGHT IS YOUR ENEMY

(Conversations with U.G. Krishnamurti)

Foreword by Mahesh Bhatt

148 pages, 140 × 215 mm

ISBN No: 81-87967-11-0

This book is a compilation of discussions between U. G. Krishnamurti and various questioners in India, Switzerland, Australia, Netherlands and U.K. According to U.G., "The religious states of bliss and ecstasy can never be experienced, can never be grasped, contained, much less given expression to, by any man. That beaten track will lead you nowhere. There is no oasis situated yonder; you are stuck with a mirage."

ETERNAL STORIES FROM THE UPANISHADS

(By Thomas Egenes & Kumuda Reddy)

199pages, 140 × 215 mm

ISBN No: 81-87967-07-2

The Upanishads include some of the most beloved and illuminating stories from the vast literature of India's Vedic tradition. Adapted from the original text, these tales tell the story of enlightenment in simple, poetic language that will appeal to all. The power and beauty of Vedic life unfolds in a variety of settings: a teacher and his student in a secluded forest ashram, a great seer meditating in a Himalayan retreat, and a proud king bowing to the wisdom of the poor. The Upanishads express the full glory of the inner Self. When one has realized the Self, everyone and every thing becomes near and dear, and one flows in universal love. This is the reality of the highest level of consciousness and the ultimate truth of life. The timeless and universal wisdom expressed in these stories reminds us of the natural flow of life towards its supreme goal.